PASTA

COOKBOOK

A Pasta Cookbook for Your Gathering

(Unlocking Appetizing Recipes in the Best Pasta Cookbook!)

Michael Roman

Published by Alex Howard

© **Michael Roman**

All Rights Reserved

Pasta Cookbook: A Pasta Cookbook for Your Gathering (Unlocking Appetizing Recipes in the Best Pasta Cookbook!)

ISBN 978-1-990169-09-0

All rights reserved. No part of this guide may be reproduced in any form without permission in writing from the publisher except in the case of brief quotations embodied in critical articles or reviews.

Legal & Disclaimer

The information contained in this book is not designed to replace or take the place of any form of medicine or professional medical advice. The information in this book has been provided for educational and entertainment purposes only.

The information contained in this book has been compiled from sources deemed reliable, and it is accurate to the best of the Author's knowledge; however, the Author cannot guarantee its accuracy and validity and cannot be held liable for any errors or omissions. Changes are periodically made to this book. You must consult your doctor or get professional medical advice before using any of the suggested remedies, techniques, or information in this book.

Table of contents

Part 1 1

Introduction 2

10 Easy Ways For Frugal Vegetarian Living 2

1. Grow Your Own Produce 2

2. Create Meal Plans And Shopping Lists 2

3. Diy 3

4. Make Use Of Leftovers 3

5. Create Dishes With Available Goods 4

6. Think Of Alternatives 4

7. Freezer Meals 4

8. Make Ahead 5

9. Purchase Goods With Long Shelf Life In Bulk 5

10. Condiments, Sauces, And Spices 5

Frugal Vegetarian Recipes 7

Hearty Vegetable Lasagna 7

Artichoke Spinach Lasagna 11

Caramelized Onion Lasagna 14

Cheese Ravioli Lasagna	18
Butternut Squash And Spinach Lasagna	21
Spinach Cheese Manicotti	25
Sesame Noodles	28
Zucchini Alfredo	30
Eggplant Pomodoro Pasta	32
Creamy Garlic Mushroom Spaghetti With Herbs	35
Healthy One Pan Penne With Broccoli	38
Easy Spinach Parmesan Pasta	41
Vegetarian Lasagna Skillet	43
Pesto Artichoke Pasta	45
Healthy Pesto Tomato And Broccoli Pasta	48
Creamy Mushroom Fettuccine	51
Zucchini And Lemon Spaghetti	54
Vegetarian Bolognese	56
Creamy Spinach Tomato Tortellini	59
Healthy Pesto-Baked Rigatoni	62
Conclusion	65

Part 2 66

Vegetarian Pasta Sauces 67

5minute Vegan Pesto 67

Amazing Greek Pasta 69

Arrabbiata Sauce 71

Basic Spicy Tomato Sauce 73

Bolognese On A Budget 74

Cilantro Jalapeno Pesto With Lime 76

Darins Vegetable Spaghetti Sauce 78

Delicious Vegetarian Bolognese 80

Easy Pesto 82

Easy Pizza Sauce I 84

Easy Tomato Sauce 85

Easy Vegan Pasta Sauce 87

Eggplant Spaghetti Sauce 88

Fried Tomato Onion And Mushroom Ragout 90

Garlic Butter Sauce I 92

Gorgonzola Cheese Sauce 93

Grandma Maggios Spaghetti Sauce 94

Grandma Rosies Extra Smooth Spaghetti Sauce 96

Heartburnfree Tomato Sauce With Kefir 97

Homemade Spaghetti Sauce 99

Homemade Tomato Sauce I 101

Instant Pot Quick And Easy Spaghetti Sauce 103

Italian Sauce 105

Lentil Bolognese 107

Moms Best Spaghetti Sauce 109

Nannys Spaghetti Sauce 111

Pasta Primavera Sauce 113

Pasta Sauce Vegan 115

Pasta With Roasted Eggplant Sauce 117

Pastapizza Sauce 119

Peanut Sauce Ii 121

Penne With Vegan Arrabbiata Sauce 123

Pepper And Olive Pasta Sauce 124

Pesto Del Sol 126

Pesto With Arugula 128

Pomodoro Pasta Sauce 130

Portobello Mushroom Bolognese Sauce 132

Presto Vegan Pesto... 134

Proper Pesto 135

Puttanesca Ii 137

Quick Pasta Sauce... 139

Roasted Tomato Sauce 140

Salsa Di Noci 142

Seven Ingredient Tomato Sauce.. 144

Sicilian Lentil Pasta Sauce 146

Simple Arrabbiata Sauce 148

Simple Garlic And Basil Pesto 149

Slow Cooker Spaghetti Sauce I 151

Spaghetti Sauce Ii 153

Spaghetti Sauce With Cauliflower 155

Spaghetti Sauce With Fresh Tomatoes 157

Sugo Di Pomodoro Authentic Italian Tomato Sauce 158

Sundried Tomato Pesto 160

Tamras Lemon Artichoke Pesto 162

The Very Best Spaghetti Sauce 164

Tomato Juice Spaghetti Sauce 166

Tomato Sauce 168

Vegan Lemon Arugula Pesto 170

Vegan Melanzane Eggplant Pasta Sauce 172

Vegan Mushroom Bolognese 174

Vegan Squash Pesto 176

Vegan Sundried Tomato Pesto 177

White Wine And Garlic Dream Cream 178

Yummy Vegan Pesto Classico 180

Chapter 6: Amazing And Tasty Pasta Sauces 182

Amazing Sundried Tomato Cream Sauce 182

Artichoke Spinach Pasta Sauce 184

Beef And Eggplant Sauce For Pasta 186

Part 1

Introduction

This book contains easy ways to be a frugal vegetarian for the pasta lover. Other than how to lower the expenses in preparing dishes, tips are also provided on how to reduce the cooking time and revamp the recipes into a gluten free or low carb dishes. The recipe selection itself consists of delicious, appetizing and wholesome dishes.

10 Easy Ways For Frugal Vegetarian Living

1. Grow Your Own Produce

This is an excellent way to start your frugal vegetarianism. Growing your own produce and herbs helps a lot in saving money from purchasing goods at grocery stores, and consistent freshness of produce is ensured. You can also avoid purchasing goods that contain toxic substances from pesticides and fertilizers. There is also less wastage because you can use the skin or peel from vegetables and fruits which are not recommended with non-organic goods. Nutritional status is also improved because most of the nutrients from vegetables and fruits are found in the skin.

2. Create Meal Plans And Shopping Lists

Creating dishes and meals plan helps a lot in vegetarianism. Due to restricted foods in the diet, vegetarians can replace it with other ingredients. By also creating new versions of dishes, it provides more choices of food to eat using limited food groups that are allowed on the diet.

Creating meal plans and shopping lists reduce wastage and helps you save time and effort from purchasing ingredients regularly at grocery stores. Creating weekly meal plans can reduce leftovers. You can make a week meal plan with dishes that use similar ingredients so you can purchase it in bulk. Purchasing goods in bulk is a frugal way because larger quantities of goods are always cheaper.

Make your shopping list after creating your weekly meal plan. This will help you in estimating the total cost of goods to purchase. If the total cost exceeds your budget, then you can make changes in the quantities or ingredient types in order to fit in your budget. Doing a shopping list also helps you save money by checking what ingredients you have and then make changes in the shopping list.

3. Diy

Do-it-yourself is always linked with saving money by using own ingredients especially those purchased in bulk. Making your own sauce, dips and marinades generally cost less than ready-made varieties. You can also adjust the flavors according to your preference and make sure it is healthy and can store them for many days.

4. Make Use Of Leftovers

It is not recommended to always have leftovers after meals. But if you have some leftover foods like bean, chilies, rice, pasta, fruits and vegetables, use them for your next dish to prepare. You can puree them and use it as a filling or sauce. Fruits can be caramelized or pureed and used as fillings in baking. Breads can be toasted to make bread crumbs or croutons. There are a lot of ways to use leftover meals, just use your creativity and passion for cooking.

5. Create Dishes With Available Goods

Every time you create a meal plan, always check the goods that you have. Make use of goods that were purchased first that than the ones that were just purchased recently. This will help to maintain the freshness of goods and reducing wastage from rotten or decomposed produce.

6. Think Of Alternatives

If the ingredient or product that you need is unavailable or expensive, think of alternatives and purchase it in the same store so that you will not go to another one. Choose alternatives that belong to the same type, like replacing spinach with kale, bok choy or other leafy greens. Also if you have purchased large quantities of seasonal produce which are very cheap like potatoes, use this as an alternative for pasta or use it instead of rice in your dishes. Vegetable spiralizers are already widely used to create vegetables into noodle spirals or different forms of pastas.

7. Freezer Meals

One way to save time and money is to prepare meals that you can freeze and just reheat it before serving. You can cook dishes in larger quantities and just place them in individual servings and in separate containers. This allows you to save time and energy in preparing your daily meals.

8. Make Ahead

This cooking preparation is also helpful in reducing the time in preparing ingredients ahead for future use. If you are cooking a dish for the day and it requires a sauce, prepare the sauce in a larger quantity and just store it in the freezer for future use. This can also be used with other ingredients like beans, vegetables, and fruits. Just store them in individual containers and label the time that it was prepared so you can use the item that was stored first.

9. Purchase Goods With Long Shelf Life In Bulk

Purchasing goods in larger quantities are always cheaper. Only buy goods that have long shelf life like grains and flours and the type of goods that are consumed in larger quantities. It is also not thrifty when you buy large quantities of goods and your consumption is very small. It is be better to purchase more on the goods what you need for the week.

10. Condiments, Sauces, And Spices

Purchasing in large quantities or making your own condiments, sauces and spices is better in large quantities. These products are always used and can be stored for many days. In vegetarianism, ingredients that add flavor are needed so that your prepared dish will be taste appetizing and will not taste bland.

Frugal Vegetarian Recipes

Hearty Vegetable Lasagna

Preparation time: 25 minutes

Cooking time: 50 to 55 minutes

Serves: 6

INGREDIENTS:

- ½ pound of lasagna sheets
- 1 cup sliced fresh mushrooms
- ½ cup chopped green bell pepper
- ½ cup chopped white onion
- 2 cloves garlic, minced
- 2 tablespoons of olive or vegetable oil
- 1 ½ cups of pasta sauce
- 1 tablespoon chopped fresh basil
- Salt and pepper, to taste
- 1 cup whole milk Ricotta cheese
- 2 cups of shredded mozzarella cheese

- 1 medium whole egg

- ½ cup grated Parmesan cheese

DIRECTIONS:

1. Preheat the oven to 350°F (175°C). Lightly grease a 9x3 inch baking dish and set aside.

2. In a large pot with boiling water, cook the lasagna pasta for about 8 to 10 minutes or until al dente. Rinse with cool running water and drain.

3. In a large pan, apply medium-high heat and add the oil. Once the oil is hot, sauté the onions and garlic for 3 minutes or until fragrant. Stir in the bell peppers and mushrooms, sauté for about 3 minutes or until the vegetables are soft and tender. Pour in the pasta sauce and add the basil and bring it to a boil. Reduce to low heat and simmer for 15 minutes and season to taste with salt and pepper.

4. In a large bowl, mix together the eggs, ricotta cheese and 1 cup of mozzarella cheese. Set aside.

5. Add ½ cup of pasta sauce in the prepared baking dish and spread evenly on the bottom. Layer half of the cooked lasagna pasta and top with half of the ricotta-mozzarella mixture.

6. Add another ½ cup of the pasta sauce, spread evenly and layer the remaining lasagna pasta. Add a layer of the remaining ricotta-mozzarella mixture. Sprinkle with grated Parmesan cheese and add the remaining sauce. Finally top with the

reserved mozzarella cheese and bake it in the oven for about 35 to 40 minutes.

7. When the vegetable lasagna is done, remove the baking dish from the oven and let it rest for 10 minutes before serving.

Nutrition Facts (per serving)

Calories: 606.5

Protein: 33g

Fat: 38.75g

Carbs: 38g

Fiber: 6g

Sugar: 8.75g

Tips:

For a Low Carb and Gluten free version of this pasta dish, replace the lasagna pasta with the shredded or sliced zucchini. Use a mandolin or vegetable spiralizer to form the zucchini into wide and thin strips. You can also use a knife in slicing the zucchini. Just slice the zucchini lengthwise starting from one end to the other, and form it into ¼-inch or ½-inch thick long strips.

Lightly salt the zucchini and place it in a colander or strainer to drain the water from the zucchini. Pat the zucchini to dry with paper towels before using it. This is important to avoid a soggy dish after baking. And also reduce the amounts of the cheeses to have a balance of flavors in preparing the dish.

Artichoke Spinach Lasagna

Preparation time: 20 minutes

Cooking time: 50 to 60 minutes

Serves: 4

INGREDIENTS:

- Olive oil or cooking spray, for greasing
- 6 lasagna sheets
- 1 medium red onion, diced
- 2 cloves garlic, minced
- 1 cup of homemade vegetable stock
- Salt and pepper, to taste
- 1 teaspoon dried rosemary leaves
- 2 cups of marinated artichoke hearts in can, drained and chopped
- 1 cup packed fresh spinach, coarsely chopped
- 1 ½ cups of pasta or tomato sauce
- 1 ½ cups shredded mozzarella cheese
- ½ cup of feta or any soft cheese

DIRECTIONS:

1. Preheat the oven to 350°F, lightly coat a 9x13 inch baking dish with oil or cooking spray and set aside.

2. In a large pot of boiling water, cook the lasagna pasta for about 8 to 10 minutes or until al dente. Rinse with cool running water and drain. Set aside.

3. In a large skillet, apply medium-high heat and lightly coat with oil or cooking spray. Sauté the garlic and onions for 3 minutes, or until soft and fragrant. Add the rosemary and the broth and bring it to a boil. Add the artichokes hearts and spinach and return to a boil, reduce to low heat. Simmer for 5 minutes and season to taste with salt and black pepper. Stir in the pasta sauce and cook until it returns to a steady simmer. Remove from heat and set aside.

4. Add ¼ of the artichoke-spinach mixture in the prepared baking dish and spread evenly on the bottom. Layer 3 cooked lasagna pasta and top with half of the shredded mozzarella. Divide the remaining artichoke-spinach mixture into two portions and add half of it into the baking dish. Layer the remaining cooked pasta over the vegetable mixture and add with the remaining shredded mozzarella. Finally add the remaining artichoke-spinach mixture and sprinkle over with crumbled feta cheese.

5. Cover with foil and bake it in the oven for 35 minutes. Remove the foil and bake for another 10 to 15 minutes or until it starts to bubble and the cheese has melted.

6. Remove from the oven and let it rest for 10 minutes before serving.

Nutrition Facts (per serving)

Calories: 363.7

Protein: 20.25g

Fat: 15.75g

Carbs: 35.25g

Fiber: 5.5g

Sugar: 8.75g

Tips:

Use butternut squash instead of lasagna pasta for a healthier dish and great for Low Carb and Gluten-free Diet. Use a mandolin, vegetable spiralizer or vegetable peeler to form the butternut squash into wide and thin strips. While preheating the oven, precook the squash for 10 minutes when the oven has reached 350°F.

Caramelized Onion Lasagna

Preparation time: 15 minutes

Active Time: 1 hour 10 minutes

Serves: 6

INGREDIENTS:

- 9 sheets of whole wheat lasagna pasta
- 3 tablespoons of olive oil
- 2 large white onions, thinly sliced
- 3 medium Portobello mushroom caps, trimmed and diced
- ½ cup red wine
- Salt and ground black pepper, to taste

For the Filling

- 3 cups loosely packed baby spinach
- 1 cup of Ricotta cheese
- ½ cup chopped fresh basil
- ½ teaspoon salt

For the Sauce and Topping

- 2 tablespoons extra-virgin olive oil
- 2 tablespoons of flour
- 1 cup whole milk
- ½ teaspoon salt
- ½ cup soft cheese
- ½ cup chopped walnuts
- ¼ cup chopped fresh basil

DIRECTIONS:

1. In a large pot with boiling water, cook the lasagna pasta for about 8 minutes or until al dente. Rinse with cool running water and drain. Set aside.

For the Onion Filling

2. In a large skillet, apply medium-low heat and add the oil. Once the oil is hot, add the onions with 1 pinch of salt. Sauté for 20 minutes or until the onions are soft and caramelized while stirring regularly. Add the mushrooms and cook until the mushrooms are soft while stirring occasionally. Pour in the wine and cook for about 3 minutes, or until the wine has completely evaporated and absorbed. Season with black pepper, remove the skillet from heat and set aside.

For the Spinach Filling

3. Place all ingredients for the spinach filling in a food processor and process until a smooth consistency is achieved. Transfer in a bowl and set aside.

For the Sauce

4. Add the oil into the saucepan over medium-high heat. Add the flour and cook until lightly golden while stirring regularly. Stir in the milk and salt, bring it to a boil while whisking regularly. Add the soft cheese and cook while stirring constantly until the cheese has melted. Remove the sauce pan from heat and set aside.

For Assembling and Baking

5. Preheat the oven to a temperature of 375°F. Lightly coat a 9x3 inch baking dish with oil or cooking spray.

6. Pour half of the milk-cheese mixture on the prepared baking dish and layer half of the cooked lasagna pasta over the sauce. Add half of the spinach filling then add half of the onion-mushroom mixture on top.

7. For the next batch of layers, start by adding the remaining cooked lasagna pasta and spread the remaining spinach filling. Top with the onion-mushroom mixture and cover with the remaining milk-cheese sauce.

8. Top with chopped walnuts and basil and bake it in the oven for about 30 minutes or until it starts to bubble. Remove the baking dish from the oven and let it rest for about 15 minutes before serving.

Nutrition Facts (per serving)

Calories: 550.7

Protein: 21.5g

Fat: 29g

Carbs: 59g

Fiber: 8.3g

Sugar: 2.1g

Tips:

Substitute the lasagna pasta with zucchini to balance the delicate taste of the zucchini with the rich and sharp flavors from the cheeses. Form the zucchini into wide and thin strips with a mandolin or vegetable peeler starting from one end to the other. You can also use a vegetable spiralizer to have a better presentation of the dish.

Lightly salt the zucchini and place it on a colander or strainer. This is to drain excess water from the zucchini and to avoid a soggy dish due to the water content of the zucchini. Pat the zucchini to dry with paper towels before using it in the dish.

Cheese Ravioli Lasagna

Preparation time: 30 minutes

Cooking time: 40 minutes

Serves: 6

INGREDIENTS:

- 1 pound of cheese ravioli, cooked and drained
- ½ cup of grated Parmesan cheese
- 1 cup of shredded Cheddar cheese
- 1 cup of shredded mozzarella cheese
- ½ teaspoons dried parsley

For the Sauce

- 2 cups of pasta or tomato sauce
- ½ cup of homemade vegetable stock or water
- 1 ½ teaspoons of sugar
- 1 ½ teaspoons dried parsley
- ½ teaspoon of ground black pepper
- ½ teaspoon of garlic powder

- ½ teaspoon of Italian seasoning mix

DIRECTIONS:

1. Preheat the oven to reach a temperature of 350°F. Lightly grease a 9x13 inch baking pan and set aside.

2. Cook the Vegetarian cheese ravioli according to package directions, drain and set aside.

3. Combine together all pasta sauce ingredients in a mixing bowl and set aside.

4. Add 2 to 3 tablespoons of pasta sauce into the prepared baking pan and spread evenly on the bottom. Add a layer of the cooked ravioli pasta, add half of the pasta sauce and then spread evenly to cover the pasta. Sprinkle half of the grated Parmesan cheese evenly on top and top with half of the shredded Cheddar Cheese.

5. Start the second set of layers by adding the remaining ravioli pasta, add the remaining sauce and spread evenly over the pasta. Layer the remaining shredded Cheddar cheese, sprinkle with dried parsley and the remaining grated Parmesan.

6. Bake it in the oven for about 4o to 45 minutes, or until it starts to bubble and lightly golden on top. Remove from the oven and let it rest for 10 minutes before serving.

Nutrition Facts (per serving)

Calories: 213.8

Protein: 11.7g

Fat: 10.7g

Carbs: 18.8g

Fiber: 1.5g

Sugar: 6.16g

Tips:

Replace ravioli pasta with thinly sliced carrots and parsnips for added nutrients and lower calorie amounts. You can use a knife or mandolin to slice the vegetables into thin diagonal cuts. For a better presentation of the dish, use a vegetable spiralizer with blade attachment that forms vegetables into thin and wide spirals. Just simply follow the recipe above and substitute the cheeses with any cheaper or available type and as long as there are 2 or more varieties to use for the dish.

Butternut Squash And Spinach Lasagna

Preparation time: 30 minutes

Cook time: 40 minutes

Serves: 4

INGREDIENTS:

- 6 sheets of lasagna pasta, cooked
- 1 cup of shredded mozzarella cheese
- ½ cup of grated Parmesan cheese
- 1 teaspoon of Italian seasoning
- ½ teaspoon of Paprika
- 2 tablespoons of chopped fresh basil leaves

For the Squash Filling

- 1 cup pureed butternut squash
- ½ cup of Ricotta cheese
- ½ cup of milk
- Salt and black pepper, to taste
- 1 pinch of ground nutmeg

For the Spinach Filling

- 1 cup of blanched spinach

- ½ cup of ricotta cheese

- ½ cup of shredded mozzarella cheese

- 2 garlic cloves, minced

- Salt and black pepper, to taste

DIRECTIONS:

1. Preheat the oven to 375°F, lightly grease a baking dish and set aside.

2. Add all ingredients for the butternut squash filling in a food processor and process until smooth and well incorporated. Season to taste with salt and pepper, transfer into a bowl and set aside. If the mixture is to thick, add more milk and process until the desired consistency is achieved.

3. In a mixing bowl, add the Ricotta Cheese, Mozzarella cheese, and garlic and then mix until well combined. Add the spinach and gently toss with the cheese mixture, season to taste with salt and pepper and set aside.

4. In a pot with boiling water, cook the lasagna pasta according to package directions, drain and set aside.

5. Add 1/3 of the butternut squash filling and layer half of the lasagna pasta over the sauce. Add a layer of half the spinach filling and top with half of the shredded cheese.

6. Pour over another 1/3 of the butternut squash filling, spread evenly and layer the remaining lasagna pasta. Add a layer of the remaining spinach filling and add the other half of the shredded mozzarella.

7. Pour over the remaining 1/3 butternut squash filling and top with grated parmesan cheese. Finally, sprinkle Italian seasoning, smoked paprika and chopped basil leaves and cover the baking dish with foil.

8. Bake it in the oven for about 30 minutes, remove the foil and bake for another 10 minutes.

9. Remove from the oven and let it rest to cool before serving.

Nutrition Facts (per serving)

Calories: 413.75

Protein: 29.25g

Fat: 20.75g

Carbs: 28g

Fiber: 2.75g

Sugar: 2.25g

Tips:

Use carrots instead of butternut squash for the filling and replace the pasta with potatoes. These vegetables create unique and complementary flavors, especially with cheese. Just make the carrot puree ahead of time and chill before use. Use Russet or any large potatoes to replace the pasta and slice it into thin rounds with a mandolin or knife. Just follow the original directions with the new ingredients.

Spinach Cheese Manicotti

Preparation time: 20 minutes

Cooking time: 45 minutes

Serves: 4

INGREDIENTS:

- 1 ½ cup of Ricotta cheese
- 1 cup loosely packed spinach, chopped
- 1 medium white onion, diced
- 1 teaspoon of dried parsley leaves
- ½ coarsely ground black pepper
- ½ teaspoon of garlic powder
- 1 cup of mozzarella cheese, shredded
- ½ cup of Parmesan cheese, grated
- 2 cups of pureed roasted tomatoes or tomato sauce
- 1 cup of homemade vegetable stock or water
- ½ pound of manicotti shells

DIRECTIONS:

1. Preheat the oven to 350°F, lightly grease a 9x13 inch baking dish and set aside.

2. Combine together the spinach, onion, 1 cup of Mozzarella, ¼ cup of Parmesan and Ricotta cheese in a mixing bowl and season to taste with salt and pepper. Stuff the uncooked manicotti shells with spinach-cheese mixture, set aside.

3. Add the tomato sauce and stock in a separate mixing bowl, sprinkle with garlic powder and parsley and mix to combine.

4. Add ½ cup of sauce in the prepared baking dish and spread evenly on the bottom. Layer the stuffed manicotti in the baking dish and pour over the remaining sauce. Spread the sauce to cover the manicotti, sprinkle the remaining grated parmesan and top with shredded Mozzarella.

5. Bake it in the oven for 40 to 45 minutes, or until the pasta is cooked through and the cheese have melted. Remove from the oven and let it rest for 10 minutes before serving.

Nutrition Facts (per serving)

Calories: 569.75

Protein: 30.75g

Fat: 21.75g

Carbs: 61.5g

Fiber: 7g

Sugar: 10g

Tips:

To have healthier and cheaper ingredients for this dish, try using parsnips and carrots as manicotti shell substitute. Just peel the root vegetables and slice it into thin rounds with a mandolin or with your knife. This type of cut is called paysanne and can be in square or round shapes. You can also use over ripe tomatoes that are roasted in the oven and pureed to save money. When this produce is in season, it is cheap very cheap so it is okay to buy in large quantities and make them into tomato sauce or purees.

Sesame Noodles

Preparation time: 15 minutes

Cooking time: 15 minutes

Serves: 4

INGREDIENTS:

- ½ pound linguine pasta
- ¼ cup of sliced green onions
- 1 teaspoon of toasted sesame seeds

For the Sauce

- 2 teaspoons of minced garlic
- ¼ cup of sugar
- ¼ cup of safflower oil
- ¼ cup of rice vinegar
- ¼ cup of soy sauce
- 1 ½ tablespoons of toasted sesame oil
- ½ tablespoon of chili sauce

DIRECTIONS:

1. In a large pot with boiling water, cook the pasta according to package directions. Drain and set aside.

2. Mix together all sauce ingredients in a saucepan and apply medium heat and cook for 5 minutes, while stirring constantly until the sugar is completely dissolves.

3. Portion the pasta into individual serving bowls, drizzle over with sauce and toss to evenly coat the pasta and serve immediately.

Nutrition Facts (per serving)

Calories: 286

Protein: 4.75g

Fat: 13.25g

Carbs: 40g

Fiber: 1.5g

Sugar: 18.75g

Tips:

Use butternut squash instead of linguini pasta, but a vegetable spiralizer is required to form the squash into elliptical noodles. Use the blade attachment that forms the vegetables into long elliptical noodles. Just blanch the spiralized squash before adding it into the dish.

Zucchini Alfredo

Preparation time: 15 minutes

Cooking time: 15 minutes

Serves: 4

INGREDIENTS:

- ½ pound of whole wheat noodles/pasta

- 2 tablespoons of vegetable oil

- 2 cloves garlic, minced

- 2 medium zucchini, diced

- ½ cup of milk

- ½ cup of cream cheese, crumbled

- ¼ cup fresh basil leaves, minced

- Salt and ground black pepper, to taste

- ¼ cup of grated Parmesan cheese

DIRECTIONS:

1. In a large pot with boiling water, cook the pasta according to package directions. Drain and set aside.

2. In a skillet, apply medium heat and add the oil. Once the oil is hot, sauté the garlic for 2 minutes and stir in the diced zucchinis. Cook for about 6 minutes or until the zucchini is soft.

3. Pour in the milk and cream cheese, season with salt and pepper and bring to a boil. Stir in the basil and parmesan and remove from heat.

4. Toss in the noodles and portion into individual serving bowls or plates.

Nutrition Facts (per serving)

Calories: 371

Protein: 15g

Fat: 41.25g

Carbs: 48.5g

Fiber: 8.25g

Sugar: 2.75g

Tips:

The perfect substitute for the pasta is parsnip spirals. You can also spiralize the zucchini for a uniform and better presentation of the dish. The flavour and crunchy texture from the parsnip complements well with the other ingredients which make this dish very appetizing and healthy as well.

Eggplant Pomodoro Pasta

Preparation time: 15 minutes

Cooking time: 35 minutes

Serves: 4

INGREDIENTS:

- 1 ½ tablespoons of olive oil
- 1 eggplant, diced
- 1 teaspoon of minced garlic
- 3 ripe red tomatoes, diced
- ¼ cup pitted green olives, sliced
- 2 tablespoons of red wine vinegar
- ¼ cup of capers
- ½ teaspoon of salt
- ½ teaspoon of coarsely ground black pepper
- 2 pinches of crushed red pepper flakes
- ½ pound of whole wheat angel hair pasta
- 3 tablespoons of minced fresh parsley leaves

DIRECTIONS:

1. In a pot with boiling water, cook the pasta according to package directions. Drain and set aside.

2. In a skillet, apply medium heat and add the oil. Add the eggplant and cook for about 5 minutes or until soft, and stir in the garlic. Cook for 1 minute, stir in the tomatoes, capers, vinegar, salt, pepper and crushed red pepper flakes. Cook until the tomatoes are soft or for about 5 minutes.

3. Toss in the past and portion into individual serving bowls. Top with parsley or basil if desired and serve.

Nutrition Facts (per serving)

Calories: 458.25

Protein: 34.25g

Fat: 15.75g

Carbs: 164.25g

Fiber: 22.5g

Sugar: 15.25g

Tips:

For this dish, zucchini spiral is an excellent substitute for angel hair pasta. A vegetable spiralizer is required to form the zucchini into thin and long spirals. But if you don't have one, you can just slice it into long and thin strands. Sprinkle with a pinch of salt before using it to drain excess water from the zucchini. This is to avoid a soggy dish due to the water contents of the zucchini.

Creamy Garlic Mushroom Spaghetti With Herbs

Preparation time: 10 minutes

Cooking time: 15 to 20 minutes

Serves: 4

INGREDIENTS:

- ½ pound whole wheat long pasta
- ¼ cup of softened butter
- 1 ½ teaspoons of minced garlic
- 1 pound of quartered mushrooms
- 2 tablespoons of flour
- 1 ½ cups milk
- Salt and coarsely ground black pepper, to taste
- 1 teaspoon mixed Italian herbs
- 2 tablespoons of olive oil
- ¼ cup minced fresh parsley leaves

DIRECTIONS:

1. In a pot with boiling water, cook the pasta according to package directions. Drain and set aside.

2. Melt 2 tablespoons of butter into a skillet over medium heat. Sauté half of the garlic for 1 minutes and stir in the mushrooms. Cook for about 6 minutes or until soft, transfer into a bowl and set aside.

3. Add the remaining butter in the same skillet and sauté the remaining garlic. Cook for 1 minute, stir in the flour and Italian herbs. Cook until the flour is lightly brown and gradually pour in the milk, bring to a boil while stirring regularly and season with salt and pepper.

4. Add the mushrooms and olive oil into the bowl with the pasta. Gently toss to coat the pasta and portion into individual serving bowls.

5. Pour over the sauce into each bowl, sprinkle with parsley and serve.

Nutrition Facts (per serving)

Calories: 372.25

Protein: 13g

Fat: 15.5g

Carbs: 47.5g

Fiber: 7.25g

Sugar: 6.25g

Tips:

You can substitute the sauce ingredients with homemade white sauce if you have it in the fridge. Basic sauces and stocks are important if you want to save time and money in preparing daily meals.

Another great tip is to freeze vegetables in separate containers that are already sliced or chopped to save time in prepping for future meals. But you must wash and peel it first before freezing. Freezing can also help in retaining the flavor and nutrients in the vegetables.

Healthy One Pan Penne With Broccoli

Preparation time: 15 minutes

Cooking time: 20 minutes

Serves: 4

INGREDIENTS:

- 1 small onion, minced
- 1 ½ teaspoons of minced garlic
- 1 tablespoon of olive oil
- 1 cup of tomato sauce
- 2 cups homemade vegetable stock or water
- ½ tablespoon dried thyme leaves
- ½ teaspoon of salt
- ½ teaspoon of ground black pepper
- ½ pound of whole wheat penne pasta
- 2 cups of detached broccoli florets
- 1 cup of shredded Mozzarella cheese
- ½ cup of minced fresh basil leaves

DIRECTIONS:

1. In a skillet, apply medium-high heat and add the oil. Sauté the garlic and onion for 4 minutes or until soft and fragrant. Stir in the tomato sauce, thyme, salt, pepper and water and pour in the stock. Add the pasta, cover with a lid and bring it to a boil. Reduce to low heat and simmer for about 10 minutes or until the pasta is cooked through.

2. Stir in the cheese and broccoli florets and cook until the cheese has melted and the broccoli is tender. Remove skillet from heat and stir in the basil.

3. Portion into individual serving bowls and serve warm.

Nutrition Facts (per serving)

Calories: 262.75

Protein: 13.25g

Fat: 10.5g

Carbs: 31.5g

Fiber: 6.25g

Sugar: 6g

Tips:

Vegetable stock is great whenever a recipe requires water. It adds flavor to your dish, and also very economical because you can use peelings and waste cuts from prepping vegetables. Just add the peelings and waste cuts of vegetables in a pot with water. Boil it for an hour and strain the liquid to have a clear stock. Discard the solids and freeze the stock for future use.

Easy Spinach Parmesan Pasta

Preparation time: 5 minutes

Cooking time: 10 minutes

Serves: 4

INGREDIENTS:

- ½ pound of whole wheat pasta
- 2 tablespoons of softened butter
- 1 teaspoon of minced garlic
- 4 cups of chopped baby spinach
- 1 cup of grated Parmesan cheese
- Salt and coarsely ground pepper, to taste

DIRECTIONS:

1. In a pot with boiling water, cook the pasta according to package directions. Drain, reserve ½ cup of cooking liquid and set aside.

2. Melt the butter in a skillet over medium heat. Add the garlic, sauté for 2 minutes and stir in the spinach. Cook until the spinach is wilted and stir in the reserved cooking liquid and ½ of the Parmesan cheese. Season with salt and pepper and toss in the pasta.

3. Portion into individual serving bowls, top with remaining Parmesan cheese and serve immediately.

Nutrition Facts (per serving)

Calories: 286.25

Protein: 12.25g

Fat: 6g

Carbs: 45.5g

Fiber: 5.75g

Sugar: 2.75g

Tips:

Substitute the pasta with spiralized potatoes or parsnips. Just blanch the vegetables first before using it. Blanching is a cooking technique to which vegetables are boiled briefly before adding it into a dish. This is to cook the vegetables evenly especially in sautéing. It also retains the crisp texture of the vegetable by only cooking it briefly.

Vegetarian Lasagna Skillet

Preparation time: 30 minutes

Cooking time: 15 to 20 minutes

Serves: 4

INGREDIENTS:

- ½ pound of bowtie pasta

- 1 ½ tablespoons of olive/canola oil

- 2 medium zucchini, diced

- 1 cup white beans, drained and rinsed

- 2 cups of homemade white pasta sauce

- ½ teaspoon garlic powder

- 1 cup of canned roasted tomatoes, drained well

- 1 cup of shredded Mozzarella cheese

DIRECTIONS:

1. In a pot with boiling water, cook the pasta according to package directions. Drain and set aside.

2. In a skillet, add the oil and apply medium heat-high heat. Add the zucchini and garlic, and cook for about 5 minutes. Stir in the beans and white pasta sauce, and cook until it reaches a boil.

Add the pasta and tomatoes, and gently toss to combine. Top with grated Mozzarella, cover and reduce heat to low. Cook for about 3 to 4 minutes or until the cheese has melted.

3. Serve immediately or portion into individual serving plates.

Nutrition Facts (per serving)

Calories: 467.5

Protein: 20.25g

Fat: 23.5g

Carbs: 45.75g

Fiber: 5.75g

Sugar: 2.75g

Tips:

To save time and money, make the white pasta sauce from scratch in advance and just store them in the fridge. Or if a recipe calls for this sauce, double the ingredients and store half for future use.

If you have a vegetable spiralizer with a blade attachment that forms vegetables into ribbons, use it to substitute the bowtie pasta with parsnips that are spiralized into ribbons. The finished dish will surely look nice and very delicious as well.

Pesto Artichoke Pasta

Preparation time: 15 minutes

Cooking time: 10 minutes

Serves: 4

INGREDIENTS:

- 2 cups of canned artichokes hearts
- 3 tablespoons of chopped fresh basil leaves
- 2 tablespoons of olive oil
- 2 lemons, juiced
- ¼ cup of vegetable stock
- ½ cup of chopped almonds
- 1 garlic clove, minced
- ½ pound of whole wheat pasta
- 1 cup of cherry tomatoes, chopped
- Salt and ground pepper, to taste

DIRECTIONS:

1. In a pot with boiling water, cook the pasta according to package directions. Drain and set aside.

2. In a skillet, add the oil and apply medium-high heat. Add the artichokes and half of lemon juice, season with salt and pepper and cook for 6 minutes while stirring occasionally. Remove skillet from heat and set aside.

3. Add the remaining lemon juice, garlic, almonds and the remaining olive oil into a food processor and pulse until a smooth sauce is achieved. Add about ¼ cup of vegetable stock if the mixture is too thick and pulse again to combine. Add the artichokes and pulse further until smooth and well incorporated.

4. Transfer into a large bowl, stir in the cherry tomatoes and season with salt and pepper if needed. Add the pasta and toss to coat with the sauce.

5. Portion into individual serving bowls or plates and serve immediately.

Nutrition Facts (per serving)

Calories: 304.25

Protein: 13.25g

Fat: 5.25g

Carbs: 58.25g

Fiber: 11.5g

Sugar: 5g

Tips:

Spiralized potatoes can be used as pasta substitute for this dish, or any vegetables that are firm and with a crunchy texture. Use a spiralizer with a blade attachment that forms vegetables into noodles and blanch it before adding into the dish.

Healthy Pesto Tomato And Broccoli Pasta

Preparation time: 15 minutes

Cooking time: 20 minutes

Serves: 4 to 6

INGREDIENTS:

- ½ pound of whole wheat pasta
- 1 teaspoon minced garlic
- 1 tablespoon olive oil
- 1 cup of homemade vegetable stock
- 1 cup ready-made pesto sauce
- 2 cups cherry tomatoes, cut in halves
- 4 cups of detached broccoli florets
- ½ cup of grated Parmesan cheese
- ½ teaspoon of salt
- ½ teaspoon of ground pepper
- 1 pinch of crushed red pepper flakes

DIRECTIONS:

1. In a pot with boiling water, cook the pasta according to package directions. Drain and set aside.

2. In a skillet, apply medium-high heat and add the oil. Sauté the garlic for 1 minute and add the pesto sauce and half of the tomatoes. Cook for about 5 minutes while stirring occasionally. Transfer into a bowl and set aside.

3. In the same skillet, add 2 tablespoons of pesto sauce, broccoli, remaining tomatoes, salt, pepper, red pepper flakes and stock and bring to a boil. Add the pasta, remove from heat and gently toss to combine.

4. Serve immediately with grated Parmesan on top or portion into individual serving plates.

Nutrition Facts (per serving)

Calories: 612.75

Protein: 24.75g

Fat: 38g

Carbs: 44.75g

Fiber: 8.25g

Sugar: 3.75g

Tips:

To retain the crunchiness of the broccoli, blanch it in a pot with boiling water and immediately transfer into a bowl with ice bath.

Submerging it in ice bath stops the cooking process to retain its texture and avoid overcooking of vegetables.

Creamy Mushroom Fettuccine

Preparation time: 10 minutes

Cooking time: 20 minutes

Serves: 4

INGREDIENTS:

- ½ pound of fettuccine pasta
- 2 tablespoons of softened butter
- 1 teaspoon of minced garlic
- 1 pound sliced Cremini mushrooms
- ½ cup diced onions
- ½ teaspoon of dried thyme leaves
- ½ teaspoon of dried dill
- Salt and crushed black pepper, to taste
- 2 tablespoons of flour
- 1 cup of homemade vegetable stock
- 1 cup cream
- 2 cups loosely packed baby spinach, chopped

- ½ cup of grated Parmesan cheese

- 2 tablespoons of mince fresh parsley leaves

DIRECTIONS:

1. In a large pot with boiling water, cook the pasta according to package instructions. Drain and set aside.

2. In a skillet, apply medium heat and melt the butter. Add the garlic, onions and mushrooms and cook for about 4 minutes or until soft and fragrant. Season with salt and pepper and stir in the thyme. Stir in the flour and cook until lightly brown and then pour in the stock and the cream. Cook until it reaches to a boil while stirring occasionally and stir in the spinach and Parmesan cheese.

3. Cook until the spinach is wilted and the cheese has melted, add the pasta and gently toss to coat the pasta evenly with the sauce.

4. Portion into individual serving bowls or plates, top with parsley and serve immediately.

Nutrition Facts (per serving)

Calories: 516.75

Protein: 21.25g

Fat: 13.5g

Carbs: 36.75g

Fiber: 6.75g

Sugar: 4.5g

Tips:

After cooking the pasta in the pot, you can also blanch the spinach for about 30 seconds and immediately submerge in a bowl with ice bath. This is to ensure even cooking of the vegetable and retains the bright shiny color of the spinach.

Spiralized potato is also a good substitute for pasta due to its firm and crunchy texture. Just blanch it a head and submerge in a bowl with an ice bath before adding into the dish.

Zucchini And Lemon Spaghetti

Preparation time: 5 minutes

Cooking time: 20 minutes

Serves: 2

INGREDIENTS:

- ½ pound wholes wheat pasta

- 3 tablespoons of olive oil

- 2 medium zucchini, diced

- 1 ½ teaspoons minced garlic

- 1 tablespoon of chopped fresh sage

- 1 tablespoon of chopped fresh rosemary leaves

- ¼ cup of grated Parmesan cheese

- ½ cup of crumbled Feta cheese

- ½ lemon, zested

- Salt and ground pepper, to taste

DIRECTIONS:

1. In a pot with boiling water, cook the pasta according to package directions. Drain and set aside.

2. In a skillet, apply medium heat and add the oil. Add the zucchini and garlic, sauté for about 5 minutes or until the zucchini is soft and tender. Stir in the fresh herbs and cook for 2 minutes while stirring regularly.

3. Stir in the lemon zest, feta cheese and ½ teaspoon of pepper and stir to combine. Add the pasta and gently toss to coat evenly with sauce.

4. Portion into individual serving bowls or plates, top with grated Parmesan and serve immediately.

Nutrition Facts (per serving)

Calories: 469

Protein: 12g

Fat: 8g

Carbs: 36.5g

Fiber: 14.5g

Sugar: 3g

Tips:

For this dish, omit the pasta and add 2 zucchinis more to have a total of 4. And form it into long and thin spirals with a spiralizer. Sprinkle with ¼ teaspoon of salt to drain excess water to have a thick and creamy sauce of the prepared dish.

Vegetarian Bolognese

Preparation time: 5 minutes

Cooking time: 15 minutes

Serves: 4

INGREDIENTS:

- 1 pound of whole wheat pasta
- 1 tablespoon of olive oil
- 1 cup diced onion
- 2 teaspoons of cloves minced garlic
- 2 tablespoons of fresh oregano leaves
- 2 tablespoons of fresh basil leaves
- 1 teaspoon of cayenne pepper
- 1 medium eggplant, diced
- 3 cups canned roasted tomatoes, pureed
- ¼ cup tomato paste
- 2 cups packed fresh spinach leaves, chopped
- 1 teaspoon crushed red pepper flakes

- Salt and ground black pepper, to taste

DIRECTIONS:

1. In a large pot with boiling water, cook the pasta according to package directions. Drain and set aside.

2. In a pan, apply medium-high heat and add the oil. Sauté the garlic and onions for 3 minute or until soft and fragrant. Add the eggplant and sprinkle with a pinch of salt. Cook for about 5 minutes while stirring regularly or until the eggplant is soft and tender.

3. Stir in the tomato sauce, fresh herbs, tomato puree and the spinach and cook until the spinach is wilted. Season to taste with salt, pepper, cayenne and crushed red pepper flakes and remove from heat.

4. Portion the pasta into individual serving bowls, pour over the sauce and serve immediately.

Nutrition Facts (per serving)

Calories: 549.25

Protein: 14g

Fat: 24.5g

Carbs: 39g

Fiber: 13.5g

Sugar: 4g

Tips:

If you prefer in using homemade and fresh ingredients in preparing dishes, make ahead different basic sauces such as tomato sauce, basic white sauce, pesto sauce and salad dressings and stored in the fridge. Tomatoes are very cheap when it is in season, so it is the perfect time to make tomato purees and sauces.

Creamy Spinach Tomato Tortellini

Preparation time: 10 minutes

Cooking time: 15 minutes

Serves: 4

INGREDIENTS:

- 1 pound three cheese tortellini
- 2 tablespoons of softened butter
- 1 teaspoon of minced garlic
- 2 tablespoons of flour
- 1 teaspoon of onion powder
- 1 cup whole milk
- ½ cup of cream
- 1 ½ cups of canned diced tomatoes
- 1 cup fresh spinach, chopped
- ¼ cup of minced fresh basil leaves
- 1 tablespoon of minced fresh oregano leaves
- Salt and coarsely ground black pepper

- ½ cup grated Parmesan cheese

- ½ teaspoon crushed red pepper flakes

DIRECTIONS:

1. In a pot with boiling water, cook the pasta according to package directions. Drain and set aside.

2. In a skillet, apply medium-high heat and melt the butter. Sauté the garlic for 1 minute and add the flour. Cook until the flour is lightly brown and add the onion powder. Pour in the milk and cream, bring to a boil while whisking regularly.

3. Stir in the tomatoes, spinach, basil, crushed red pepper flakes and oregano and then season to taste with salt and pepper. Cook until the sauce has thickened and the spinach is wilted. Stir in the Parmesan cheese and remove from heat.

4. Gently toss cooked tortellini to coat evenly with sauce and portion into individual serving bowls. Serve immediately with extra grated Parmesan on top if desired.

Nutrition Facts (per serving)

Calories: 391.75

Protein: 11.5g

Fat: 14g

Carbs: 42g

Fiber: 13.5g

Sugar: 3.75g

Tips:

Beurre manié is a French term for dough that is used to thicken sauces. It is a mixture of equal parts of softened butter and flour kneaded together to form into a dough. If you like pasta and other dishes with creamy sauces, you should always have Beurre manié in your fridge.

Compound butter is a mixture of butter, herbs and/or spices. This is used in sautéing ingredients and toppings for different dishes. To make a compound butter, finely chop and ground the herbs and spices and mix it with softened butter. Transfer it to a cling wrap or foil and roll it to form a log or cylinder and store it in the fridge for future use.

Healthy Pesto-Baked Rigatoni

Preparation time: 15 minutes

Cooking time: 25 minutes

Serves: 4

INGREDIENTS:

For the pasta:

- ½ pound of whole wheat elbow pasta
- 2 cups diced tomatoes
- ½ cup homemade vegetable stock or water
- ½ cup shredded Cheddar or Mozzarella cheese

For the Pesto Sauce

- 1 cup chopped fresh spinach
- ½ cup chopped kale
- ½ cup fresh basil leaves
- ¼ cup pine nuts
- ¼ cup of olive oil
- ¼ cup grated Parmesan cheese

- ½ teaspoon salt

- 2 garlic cloves

- 1 lemon, juiced

DIRECTIONS:

1. In a pot with boiling water, cook the pasta according to package directions. Drain and set aside.

2. Preheat the oven to 400°F and lightly grease a 9x13 inch baking dish.

3. Add all pesto ingredients in a food processor and pulse until smooth. Scrape the sides and press down the spinach to process evenly.

4. Toss in the pasta and tomatoes with the sauce and add stock if needed to adjust the consistency. Sprinkle with grated Parmesan on top and cover with foil.

5. Bake it in the oven for 15 to 18 minutes, remove from the oven and let it rest for 10 minutes before removing the foil.

6. Serve immediately.

Nutrition Facts (per serving)

Calories: 562.75

Protein: 22.25g

Fat: 36.75g

Carbs: 40g

Fiber: 9g

Sugar: 4.5g

Tips:

There are different kinds of pesto sauce for various recipe dishes. It adds rich and savory flavors to a dish with simple ingredients and taste. Since it takes some time to prepare it, you should have a premade favorite pesto sauce stored in your fridge.

Conclusion

Fresh vegetables, herbs and cheese have simple but decadent tastes and wholesomeness. And it compliments well with pasta. The tips is to balance the flavors and textures of those ingredients to create a dish with a unique taste from complementary flavors.

Remember, with your creativity and resourcefulness, simple ingredients can be turned into dishes that look and taste gourmet.

Part 2

Vegetarian Pasta Sauces

5minute Vegan Pesto

"This quick and easy vegan pesto is a delicious topping for any pizza, pasta or salad, and takes only 5 minutes with just a few ingredients."

SERVING: 6 | PREP: 5 M | READY IN: 5 M

Ingredients

- 3 cups fresh basil leaves
- 2/3 cup olive oil
- 1/4 cup pine nuts
- 2 tablespoons nutritional yeast
- 2 cloves garlic
- 1/2 teaspoon salt
- 1/4 teaspoon ground black pepper

Direction

- Combine basil leaves, olive oil, pine nuts, nutritional yeast, garlic, salt, and black pepper in the bowl of a food processor; pulse until smooth.

Nutrition Information

- Calories: 259 calories
- Total Fat: 27.1 g
- Cholesterol: 0 mg
- Sodium: 196 mg
- Total Carbohydrate: 2.6 g
- Protein: 3.4 g

Amazing Greek Pasta

"This tomato sauce combines the flavors of garlic, onion, kalamata olives capers. It is wonderful over any pasta or as a sauce for white fish or chicken."

SERVING: 4 | PREP: 15 M | COOK: 2 H | READY IN: 2 H 15 M

Ingredients

- 1 small yellow onion, diced
- 1 tablespoon olive oil
- 5 cloves garlic, minced
- 1 (16 ounce) can organic Italian diced tomatoes
- 1 (6.5 ounce) can tomato sauce
- 1 tablespoon capers, chopped
- 15 kalamata olives, pitted and sliced
- 2 tablespoons balsamic vinegar
- salt and pepper to taste
- crushed red pepper to taste (optional)
- crumbled Feta or grated Parmesan Cheese

Direction

- In a skillet, cook onion in olive oil over medium high heat until tender and translucent. Stir in garlic, and cook for 1 minute. Add tomatoes, tomato sauce, capers, olives, vinegar, salt, pepper, and crushed red pepper (if using).
- Reduce heat, cover, and simmer for a minimum of 30 minutes, or up to 2 hours, time permitting. Serve over pasta, fish, or chicken, and top with crumbled feta or grated Parmesan cheese. Enjoy!

Nutrition Information

- Calories: 205 calories
- Total Fat: 14 g
- Cholesterol: 28 mg
- Sodium: 1442 mg
- Total Carbohydrate: 12.8 g
- Protein: 6.8 g

Arrabbiata Sauce

"Spicy and delicious. Ideal on penne pasta."

SERVING: 6 | PREP: 15 M | COOK: 20 M | READY IN: 35 M

Ingredients

- 1 teaspoon olive oil
- 1 cup chopped onion
- 4 cloves garlic, minced
- 3/8 cup red wine
- 1 tablespoon white sugar
- 1 tablespoon chopped fresh basil
- 1 teaspoon crushed red pepper flakes
- 2 tablespoons tomato paste
- 1 tablespoon lemon juice
- 1/2 teaspoon Italian seasoning
- 1/4 teaspoon ground black pepper
- 2 (14.5 ounce) cans peeled and diced tomatoes
- 2 tablespoons chopped fresh parsley

Direction

- Heat oil in a large skillet or saucepan over medium heat. Sauté onion and garlic in oil for 5 minutes.
- Stir in wine, sugar, basil, red pepper, tomato paste, lemon juice, Italian seasoning, black pepper and tomatoes; bring to a boil. Reduce heat to medium, and simmer uncovered about 15 minutes.
- Stir in parsley. Ladle over the hot cooked pasta of your choice.

Nutrition Information

- Calories: 77 calories
- Total Fat: 1 g
- Cholesterol: 0 mg
- Sodium: 258 mg
- Total Carbohydrate: 11.8 g
- Protein: 1.9 g

Basic Spicy Tomato Sauce

"This sauce can be used for spaghetti, ravioli, chicken Parmesan, or anything Italian! It's very quick and very easy! Anything from seasoning to spices can be adjusted without compromising the basic flavor of the sauce. Sometimes we add bell peppers or tomatoes with green chiles. Add anything you like."

SERVING: 6 | PREP: 10 M | COOK: 10 M | READY IN: 20 M

Ingredients

- 2 tablespoons extra-virgin olive oil
- 1 cup diced onion
- 4 cloves garlic, chopped
- 1 (28 ounce) can crushed tomatoes
- 2 teaspoons crushed red pepper flakes
- 2 teaspoons Italian seasoning
- salt to taste

Direction

- Heat the olive oil in a large skillet over medium-high heat. Cook the onion in the oil until translucent. Add the garlic and cook and stir another 2 to 3 minutes. Stir in the tomatoes, red pepper flakes, and Italian seasoning. Season with salt. Cook until completely heated, another 2 to 3 minutes.

Nutrition Information

- Calories: 101 calories
- Total Fat: 5.1 g

- Cholesterol: 0 mg
- Sodium: 174 mg
- Total Carbohydrate: 13.6 g
- Protein: 2.7 g

Bolognese On A Budget

"This delicious bolognese is extremely quick and easy to make. Serve over pasta, rice, couscous, or any other carbohydrate food you fancy. This sauce gets better the longer it simmers. If you do allow it to simmer for a longer time, check regularly and add water as needed. This sauce also lends itself beautifully to adding vegetables such as zucchini, eggplant, carrots, and mushrooms."

SERVING: 4 | PREP: 5 M | COOK: 10 M | READY IN: 15 M

Ingredients

- 1 cup red lentils
- 1 3/4 cups water
- 2 (14.4 ounce) cans chopped canned tomatoes
- 2 onions, chopped
- 1 cube vegetable bouillon
- salt and ground black pepper to taste

Direction

- Rinse lentils under cold running water and drain. Place the water and lentils in a saucepan over medium heat and bring to a boil. Cover, reduce heat to medium-low, and simmer until lentils just begin to soften, about 20 minutes. Stir the tomatoes and onions into the lentils; bring to a gentle simmer. Crumble the bouillon cube into the lentil mixture and stir until it's dissolved. Simmer about 5 minutes more, stirring frequently. Season with salt and pepper to taste.

Nutrition Information

- Calories: 226 calories
- Total Fat: 0.8 g
- Cholesterol: 0 mg
- Sodium: 303 mg
- Total Carbohydrate: 42.2 g
- Protein: 14.6 g

Cilantro Jalapeno Pesto With Lime

"This is a spicy alternative to classic basil pesto. You can control the spiciness by using less jalapeno and by removing the seeds and white membrane of the pepper before adding it to the pesto. If you like the spice, just throw it all in!"

SERVING: 6 | PREP: 10 M | READY IN: 10 M

Ingredients

- 1 bunch fresh cilantro
- 2 1/2 tablespoons toasted pine nuts
- 1/4 cup extra virgin olive oil
- 5 cloves garlic
- 1 tablespoon fresh lime juice
- 1/2 fresh jalapeno pepper, seeded
- 1/4 cup grated Parmesan cheese

Direction

- Combine the cilantro, pine nuts, olive oil, garlic, lime juice, jalapeno pepper, and Parmesan cheese in a blender; pulse until the mixture reaches a soft, paste-like consistency.

Nutrition Information

- Calories: 129 calories
- Total Fat: 12.4 g
- Cholesterol: 4 mg
- Sodium: 69 mg
- Total Carbohydrate: 1.9 g

- Protein: 2.8 g

Darins Vegetable Spaghetti Sauce

"A delicious mix of veggies and cheese make for a surprisingly hearty and easy meal, despite all the chopping. I'm not a vegetarian and I can eat this as a meal without missing meat one bit! Serve on thin spaghetti or capellini."

SERVING: 6 | PREP: 30 M | COOK: 35 M | READY IN: 1 H 5 M

Ingredients

- 3/4 cup butter
- 2 cloves garlic, minced
- 1 teaspoon ground black pepper
- 2 1/2 cups diced carrots
- 2 1/2 cups diced celery
- 2 1/2 cups diced onions
- 2 (28 ounce) cans crushed tomatoes
- 1 1/2 tablespoons dried parsley, or to taste
- 1 tablespoon white sugar, or to taste
- 6 tablespoons Parmesan cheese
- 2 tablespoons cornstarch
- 1 tablespoon hot water

Direction

- Melt butter in a large pot over medium-low heat; add garlic and pepper. Cook and stir mixture until garlic is fragrant, about 3 minutes. Stir carrots, celery, and onions into the butter, increase heat to medium, and continue to cook and stir until the vegetables are tender, 5 to 7 minutes.

- Stir crushed tomatoes, parsley, and sugar into the vegetable mixture. Reduce heat to low and cook mixture at a simmer, stirring occasionally, for 20 minutes. Add Parmesan cheese and simmer to melt the cheese, about 5 minutes more.
- Whisk cornstarch into hot water in a small bowl; add to sauce. Stir the cornstarch slurry into the sauce and cook until the sauce thickens, 1 to 2 minutes more.

Nutrition Information

- Calories: 387 calories
- Total Fat: 25.5 g
- Cholesterol: 65 mg
- Sodium: 667 mg
- Total Carbohydrate: 37.3 g
- Protein: 8.2 g

Delicious Vegetarian Bolognese

"I am so excited to share this recipe with you. I've tried making vegetarian Bolognese many times but never really succeeded. This time it turned out really great and it's now one of my family's favorite meals. Lentils are not usually my daughter's favorite food but this Bolognese has been a huge success. Another plus about this recipe: it will be good the first day but even better the second day. So make a big batch and enjoy this Bolognese over a couple of days. Garnish with Parmesan cheese and serve with a salad."

SERVING: 4 | PREP: 15 M | COOK: 29 M | READY IN: 44 M

Ingredients

- 1 tablespoon vegetable oil
- 2 cups finely chopped mushrooms
- 1 cup finely chopped leek
- 2 teaspoons salt
- 1 teaspoon red pepper flakes
- coarsely ground black pepper to taste
- 1 (28 ounce) can crushed tomatoes
- 3/4 cup creme fraiche
- 2 carrots, grated
- 1/2 cup red lentils
- 3 tablespoons vegetable broth (such as Knorr® Touch of Taste)
- 1/2 teaspoon sambal oelek (chile paste)

Direction

- Heat oil in a large saucepan over medium heat. Add mushrooms, leek, salt, red pepper flakes, and pepper; cook and stir until mushrooms are soft, 5 to 10 minutes.
- Stir crushed tomatoes, creme fraiche, carrots, red lentils, vegetable broth, and sambal oelek into the saucepan. Bring to a gentle simmer. Cover and cook, stirring occasionally, until flavors combine, about 20 minutes.

Nutrition Information

- Calories: 369 calories
- Total Fat: 21.7 g
- Cholesterol: 61 mg
- Sodium: 1497 mg
- Total Carbohydrate: 38.1 g
- Protein: 12.9 g

Easy Pesto

"This is the easiest pesto recipe, using easy to find ingredients. It can be prepared in 2 minutes after you toast the almonds."

SERVING: 6 | PREP: 2 M | COOK: 10 M | READY IN: 12 M

Ingredients

- 1/4 cup almonds
- 3 cloves garlic
- 1 1/2 cups fresh basil leaves
- 1/2 cup olive oil
- 1 pinch ground nutmeg
- salt and pepper to taste

Direction

- Preheat oven to 450 degrees F (230 degrees C). Place almonds on a cookie sheet, and bake for 10 minutes, or until lightly toasted.
- In a food processor, combine toasted almonds, garlic, basil, olive oil, nutmeg, salt and pepper. Process until a coarse paste is formed.

Nutrition Information

- Calories: 199 calories
- Total Fat: 21.1 g
- Cholesterol: 0 mg
- Sodium: 389 mg
- Total Carbohydrate: 2 g

- Protein: 1.7 g

Easy Pizza Sauce I

"A simple pizza sauce used by many pizzerias. The thickness of the sauce is regulated by the amount of water used; it should be somewhat viscous."

SERVING: 8

Ingredients

- 1 (6 ounce) can tomato paste
- 1 1/2 cups water
- 1/3 cup extra virgin olive oil
- 2 cloves garlic, minced
- salt to taste
- ground black pepper to taste
- 1/2 tablespoon dried oregano
- 1/2 tablespoon dried basil
- 1/2 teaspoon dried rosemary, crushed

Direction

- Mix together the tomato paste, water, and olive oil. Mix well. Add garlic, salt and pepper to taste, oregano, basil, and rosemary. Mix well and let stand several hours to let flavors blend. No cooking necessary, just spread on dough.

Nutrition Information

- Calories: 104 calories
- Total Fat: 9.5 g
- Cholesterol: 0 mg

- Sodium: 170 mg
- Total Carbohydrate: 4.7 g
- Protein: 1 g

Easy Tomato Sauce

"Easy and yummy tomato sauce with few ingredients. Tasty."

SERVING: 4 | COOK: 30 M | READY IN: 30 M

Ingredients

- 4 tablespoons olive oil
- 1 onion, chopped
- 3 tomatoes, chopped
- 1 tablespoon tomato puree
- salt and pepper to taste

Direction

- In a large skillet over medium heat, cook onion in olive oil until translucent. Stir in tomatoes, cook until juice begins to thicken. Stir in puree, salt and pepper. Reduce heat and simmer 15 minutes more, until rich and thick.

Nutrition Information

- Calories: 204 calories
- Total Fat: 16 g
- Cholesterol: 0 mg
- Sodium: 437 mg
- Total Carbohydrate: 14.8 g

- Protein: 2.2 g

Easy Vegan Pasta Sauce

"This is the most beautiful tasting low-fat pasta sauce you'll ever taste! Don't wait to try it!"

SERVING: 3 | PREP: 15 M | COOK: 20 M | READY IN: 35 M

Ingredients

- 1 teaspoon vegetable oil
- 1/2 small yellow onion, diced
- 2 cloves garlic, minced
- 5 large tomatoes, cubed
- 1 small green bell pepper, diced
- 1/2 teaspoon salt
- 1/2 teaspoon black pepper
- 1 teaspoon dried basil leaves
- 1/2 teaspoon dried oregano

Direction

- In a skillet over medium-low heat, sauté onion and garlic in the vegetable oil. Place tomatoes into onion and garlic mixture. Stir in diced bell pepper, salt, pepper, basil and oregano. Let simmer for 20 minutes, stirring occasionally. Turn down heat if it starts to stick.

Nutrition Information

- Calories: 85 calories
- Total Fat: 2 g
- Cholesterol: 0 mg

- Sodium: 1197 mg
- Total Carbohydrate: 16 g
- Protein: 3.5 g

Eggplant Spaghetti Sauce

"This is a lovely eggplant spaghetti sauce I made one day when I was bored and just wanted an alternative to the regular red sauce. Add spaghetti to the mixture or else add spaghetti on the side. This also goes well if you add a little mozzarella or Parmesan cheese on top."

SERVING: 4 | PREP: 25 M | COOK: 30 M | READY IN: 55 M

Ingredients

- 2 ounces butter
- 2 large onions, diced
- 1 clove garlic, minced
- 1 large eggplant, peeled and cut into bite-size pieces
- 1 red bell pepper, chopped
- 1 green bell pepper, chopped
- 1 stalk celery, chopped
- 1/2 (8 ounce) package sliced baby bella mushrooms
- 1 (12 ounce) can tomato sauce

Direction

- Melt butter in a large skillet over medium heat. Add onions and garlic; cook and stir until tender, about 5 minutes. Add eggplant, red bell pepper, green bell pepper, celery, and mushrooms; cook and stir until eggplant is tender but not mushy, about 10 minutes. Pour in tomato sauce. Simmer until bubbly and thick, about 15 minutes.

Nutrition Information

- Calories: 216 calories
- Total Fat: 12.2 g
- Cholesterol: 30 mg
- Sodium: 544 mg
- Total Carbohydrate: 25.9 g
- Protein: 5.3 g

Fried Tomato Onion And Mushroom Ragout

"When I was growing up, my mother used to make a simple dish of fried tomatoes and onions that we would soak up with buttered bread. This is an updated version to which I have added mushrooms and fresh basil. My daughter loves this over whole wheat penne pasta and topped with Parmesan cheese."

SERVING: 4 | PREP: 15 M | COOK: 25 M | READY IN: 40 M

Ingredients

- 2 tablespoons olive oil
- 1 cup chopped onion
- 4 tomatoes, cut into wedges
- 2 cups sliced white mushrooms
- 1/4 cup chopped fresh basil
- salt and black pepper to taste

Direction

- Heat the olive oil in a large skillet over medium heat, and cook and stir the onion for about 5 minutes, until translucent. Add the tomato wedges and mushrooms, and simmer, stirring occasionally, for about 20 minutes, until the tomatoes and mushrooms are cooked through and the sauce is reduced and thickened.
- Sprinkle on the basil, salt and pepper, and stir to combine.

Nutrition Information

- Calories: 106 calories
- Total Fat: 7.2 g
- Cholesterol: 0 mg
- Sodium: 10 mg
- Total Carbohydrate: 9.8 g
- Protein: 2.7 g

Garlic Butter Sauce I

"A rich, buttery sauce for pasta with herbs and garlic. Great with grated Parmesan or Romano cheese. Try serving it over your favorite pasta. Easy to double or triple."

SERVING: 1

Ingredients

- 1/3 cup butter
- 1 clove crushed garlic
- 1/4 tablespoon dried basil
- 2 teaspoons dried oregano

Direction

- In a small saucepan melt butter, add garlic and sauté until cooked. Add dried oregano and dried basil and stir until heated through.
- Serve warm.

Nutrition Information

- Calories: 559 calories
- Total Fat: 61.7 g
- Cholesterol: 163 mg
- Sodium: 437 mg
- Total Carbohydrate: 3.7 g
- Protein: 1.3 g

Gorgonzola Cheese Sauce

"You can make any ordinary meal into some extraordinary with the deep, rich flavor of this Gorgonzola cheese sauce."

SERVING: 8 | PREP: 5 M | COOK: 15 M | READY IN: 20 M

Ingredients

- 3 tablespoons butter
- 3 tablespoons all-purpose flour
- 3 cups milk
- 1/3 cup crumbled Gorgonzola cheese
- 1/4 teaspoon salt
- 1/4 teaspoon black pepper

Direction

- Melt butter in a medium saucepan over medium-low heat. Stir in flour, then milk. When mixture begins to thicken, stir in cheese. Cook until cheese is melted and sauce reaches desired consistency. Season with salt and pepper.

Nutrition Information

- Calories: 120 calories
- Total Fat: 8.2 g
- Cholesterol: 26 mg
- Sodium: 211 mg
- Total Carbohydrate: 6.6 g
- Protein: 4.9 g

Grandma Maggios Spaghetti Sauce

"This is one that was recited to me out of memory alone, and described as a hand of garlic, etc., though the ingredient quantities should be accurate. I encourage buying the cheapest versions of these ingredients you can find; it will feed an army for about $15 without ruining the taste. You should add more seasonings based on preference. A great vegetarian sauce, and with meatballs...it makes great meatball sandwiches."

SERVING: 10 | PREP: 20 M | COOK: 35 M | READY IN: 55 M

Ingredients

- 2 tablespoons olive oil
- 1 onion, chopped
- 1 whole head garlic, peeled and chopped
- 2 cups sliced fresh mushrooms
- 1/2 cup chopped fresh basil leaves, or to taste
- 1 (28 ounce) can whole peeled tomatoes
- 1 (15 ounce) can tomato sauce
- 1 (6 ounce) can tomato paste
- 3/4 cup Merlot wine
- 2 teaspoons salt
- 1 teaspoon ground black pepper
- 2 teaspoons dried oregano
- 1/4 cup white sugar

Direction

- Heat olive oil in a large saucepan over medium-low heat, and cook and stir the onion and garlic until translucent but not

browned, 6 to 7 minutes. Stir in the mushrooms and basil, and cook and stir until the basil is wilted and the mushrooms are cooked through and have given up their juices, about 10 minutes.
- Pour in the whole peeled tomatoes, and bring the mixture to a boil, stirring and chopping the tomatoes into pieces with a spoon. Pour in the tomato sauce and stir, crushing any large pieces of tomato left, and bring to a simmer. Let the sauce simmer until slightly thickened and bubbling, stirring occasionally, about 15 minutes.
- Stir the tomato paste into the sauce, and fill the empty tomato paste can with Merlot wine, stirring to dissolve any remaining tomato paste in the can. Pour the Merlot wine into the sauce, and stir well to combine. Bring the sauce back to a simmer, and stir in the salt, pepper, dried oregano, and sugar. Let the sauce simmer until the seasonings are blended and the sauce is heated through, about 3 more minutes.

Nutrition Information

- Calories: 114 calories
- Total Fat: 3.1 g
- Cholesterol: 0 mg
- Sodium: 935 mg
- Total Carbohydrate: 18 g
- Protein: 3.1 g

Grandma Rosies Extra Smooth Spaghetti Sauce

"A mild sweet, super smooth pasta sauce that has become a family favorite! Makes a great sauce for meatballs. I recommend adding them and letting the entire pot simmer and meld. And remember, the bay leaf is lucky!"

SERVING: 6 | PREP: 5 M | COOK: 45 M | READY IN: 50 M

Ingredients

- 1 (46 fluid ounce) can tomato juice
- 1 (6 ounce) can tomato paste
- 2 tablespoons brown sugar
- 1 clove garlic, crushed
- 1 tablespoon dried oregano
- 3/4 teaspoon dried basil
- 1/2 teaspoon dried marjoram
- 1 bay leaf
- 3/4 teaspoon salt

Direction

- Combine tomato juice, tomato paste, brown sugar, garlic, oregano, basil, marjoram, bay leaf, and salt in a large pot. Bring to a boil, reduce heat, and cover. Simmer until thickened, about 45 minutes.

Nutrition Information

- Calories: 81 calories
- Total Fat: 0.3 g

- Cholesterol: 0 mg
- Sodium: 1094 mg
- Total Carbohydrate: 19.6 g
- Protein: 3 g

Heartburnfree Tomato Sauce With Kefir

"I'm eight months pregnant right now, and craving pasta like crazy! But traditional tomato sauce gives me wicked heartburn, so I developed this recipe with kefir. All the yumminess of tomato sauce without the burn! Serve over the pasta of your choice."

SERVING: 4 | PREP: 5 M | COOK: 25 M | READY IN: 30 M

Ingredients

- 1 tablespoon olive oil
- 2 cloves garlic
- 1 (28 ounce) can crushed tomatoes
- 2 tablespoons tomato paste
- 1 teaspoon salt, or to taste
- 1/2 teaspoon dried oregano
- 1/2 teaspoon dried thyme
- 1/4 teaspoon baking soda
- 1 cup plain kefir

Direction

- Heat olive oil in a saucepan over medium heat. Add garlic and cook until just fragrant, about 30 seconds. Add crushed tomatoes, tomato paste, salt, oregano, and thyme. Simmer until tomatoes are soft, about 10 minutes. Add baking soda and stir. Simmer until thickened, about 10 minutes more. Remove from heat and stir in kefir.

Nutrition Information

- Calories: 140 calories
- Total Fat: 6 g
- Cholesterol: 0 mg
- Sodium: 1010 mg
- Total Carbohydrate: 19.4 g
- Protein: 5.6 g

Homemade Spaghetti Sauce

"Homemade Italian spaghetti sauce from an Italian family. The longer you cook it the better it tastes."

SERVING: 6 | PREP: 10 M | COOK: 4 H | READY IN: 4 H 10 M

Ingredients

- 1 chopped onion
- 5 cloves garlic, chopped
- 2 teaspoons olive oil
- 2 (28 ounce) cans peeled ground tomatoes in paste
- 1 (6 ounce) can Italian-style tomato paste
- 7 cups water
- 3 tablespoons Italian seasoning
- 2 tablespoons dried basil
- 1 teaspoon white sugar
- 1/2 cup red wine
- 1 pinch crushed red pepper

Direction

- In large saucepan over medium heat, sauté onion and garlic in olive oil until soft. Stir in tomatoes, tomato paste, water, Italian seasoning, basil, sugar, wine, and crushed red pepper. Reduce heat to low and simmer 3 hours, stirring occasionally. Serve.

Nutrition Information

- Calories: 126 calories

- Total Fat: 2.4 g
- Cholesterol: 0 mg
- Sodium: 651 mg
- Total Carbohydrate: 20.3 g
- Protein: 5.8 g

Homemade Tomato Sauce I

"Fresh and delicious."

SERVING: 6 | PREP: 30 M | COOK: 4 H | READY IN: 4 H 30 M

Ingredients

- 10 ripe tomatoes
- 2 tablespoons olive oil
- 2 tablespoons butter
- 1 onion, chopped
- 1 green bell pepper, chopped
- 2 carrots, chopped
- 4 cloves garlic, minced
- 1/4 cup chopped fresh basil
- 1/4 teaspoon Italian seasoning
- 1/4 cup Burgundy wine
- 1 bay leaf
- 2 stalks celery
- 2 tablespoons tomato paste

Direction

- Bring a pot of water to a boil. Have ready a large bowl of iced water. Plunge whole tomatoes in boiling water until skin starts to peel, 1 minute. Remove with slotted spoon and place in ice bath. Let rest until cool enough to handle, then remove peel and squeeze out seeds. Chop 8 tomatoes and puree in blender or food processor. Chop remaining two tomatoes and set aside.

- In a large pot or Dutch oven over medium heat, cook onion, bell pepper, carrot and garlic in oil and butter until onion starts to soften, 5 minutes. Pour in pureed tomatoes. Stir in chopped tomato, basil, Italian seasoning and wine. Place bay leaf and whole celery stalks in pot. Bring to a boil, then reduce heat to low, cover and simmer 2 hours. Stir in tomato paste and simmer an additional 2 hours. Discard bay leaf and celery and serve.

Nutrition Information

- Calories: 149 calories
- Total Fat: 8.9 g
- Cholesterol: 10 mg
- Sodium: 105 mg
- Total Carbohydrate: 15 g
- Protein: 2.9 g

Instant Pot Quick And Easy Spaghetti Sauce

"This rich and tasty homemade spaghetti sauce is made with fresh tomatoes! Just what you need for any pasta dish, and so quick and easy to make in the Instant Pot®."

SERVING: 6 | PREP: 10 M | COOK: 45 M | READY IN: 1 H 5 M

Ingredients

- 2 tablespoons olive oil
- 2 yellow onions, chopped
- 2 cloves garlic, minced
- 1 carrot, chopped
- 1 celery stalk, chopped
- 3 pounds plum tomatoes
- 1 teaspoon dried oregano
- 1 teaspoon Italian seasoning
- 1 teaspoon sea salt
- 1 teaspoon dried basil
- 1/2 teaspoon ground black pepper

Direction

- Turn on a multi-functional pressure cooker (such as Instant Pot(R)) and select Sauté function. Heat olive oil and stir in onions and garlic; cook until soft and translucent, about 5 minutes. Add carrot, celery, and tomatoes; cook until tender, about 4 minutes. Season with oregano, Italian seasoning, salt, basil, and pepper. Close and lock the lid. Select high

pressure according to manufacturer's instructions; set timer for 25 minutes. Allow 10 to 15 minutes for pressure to build.
- Release pressure using the natural-release method according to manufacturer's instructions, 10 to 40 minutes. Unlock and remove the lid. Blend with an immersion blender to desired consistency.

Nutrition Information

- Calories: 125 calories
- Total Fat: 5.2 g
- Cholesterol: 0 mg
- Sodium: 351 mg
- Total Carbohydrate: 18.8 g
- Protein: 3.4 g

Italian Sauce

"This is a basic Italian sauce that can be used in any dish, including lasagne, cannelloni, ravioli, etc. It's very easy and tastes so good! Also, it smells like heaven!"

SERVING: 16 | PREP: 10 M | COOK: 20 M | READY IN: 30 M

Ingredients

- 11 tomatoes, coarsely chopped
- 1/2 cup red wine vinegar
- 1/2 cup white sugar
- 1 1/2 teaspoons paprika
- 1/2 teaspoon salt
- 1/4 teaspoon crushed garlic
- 1 tablespoon crushed red pepper
- 1 cinnamon stick
- 4 whole cloves

Direction

- Puree tomatoes in blender or food processor until smooth. Pour into a large saucepan with the red wine vinegar, sugar, paprika, salt, garlic, crushed red pepper, cinnamon stick and cloves. Simmer over medium-low heat, covered, until thickened and flavors have blended, 15 to 20 minutes. Remove cinnamon stick and cloves before serving.

Nutrition Information

- Calories: 97 calories

- Total Fat: 2.4 g
- Cholesterol: 0 mg
- Sodium: 458 mg
- Total Carbohydrate: 18.6 g
- Protein: 1.8 g

Lentil Bolognese

"Delicious vegetarian sauce for pasta, so tasty, and as nice as a meat bolognese. It can also be served with potatoes."

SERVING: 4 | PREP: 20 M | COOK: 32 M | READY IN: 52 M

Ingredients

- 1 tablespoon olive oil, or to taste
- 1 onion, finely chopped
- 2 cloves garlic, crushed and finely chopped
- 1/2 red bell pepper, thinly sliced
- 1 carrot, cut into small cubes
- 1/2 cup thinly sliced mushrooms
- 1/2 cup red wine
- 1 (14 ounce) can diced tomatoes
- 1 cup vegetable broth
- 1 (15 ounce) can green lentils, drained
- 1 teaspoon ground paprika, or more to taste
- 1 teaspoon dried basil, or more to taste
- 1 teaspoon dried oregano, or more to taste
- 1 teaspoon mixed dried herbs, or to taste
- 1 pinch ground nutmeg

Direction

- Heat olive oil in a large pot over medium heat. Cook and stir onion and garlic until soft, about 5 minutes. Stir in red bell pepper and carrot; cook for 4 to 5 minutes. Add mushrooms; cook and stir until softened, about 2 minutes.

- Pour wine into the pot; simmer until slightly reduced, about 1 minute. Stir in diced tomatoes and vegetable broth. Bring sauce to a boil; reduce heat and simmer until flavors combine, 10 to 15 minutes. Stir in lentils, paprika, basil, oregano, dried herbs, and nutmeg; cook until lentils are heated through, about 5 minutes.

Nutrition Information

- Calories: 205 calories
- Total Fat: 3.9 g
- Cholesterol: 0 mg
- Sodium: 404 mg
- Total Carbohydrate: 27.9 g
- Protein: 9.1 g

Moms Best Spaghetti Sauce

"A simple, slow cooked, authentic spaghetti sauce, as good as the restaurants serve...or better! The secret ingredient is baking soda, but do not taste the sauce right after adding it. Wait a while, and this sauce will not disappoint you. It is good right from the stove, but the flavors blend overnight. Best served with your favorite meatball recipe, where the meatballs cook in the sauce the last half hour. Be prepared to take a nap after eating."

SERVING: 8

Ingredients

- 4 (14.5 ounce) cans whole peeled tomatoes
- 2 (15 ounce) cans tomato sauce
- 4 (6 ounce) cans tomato paste
- 3 cups water
- 4 cups fresh sliced mushrooms
- 2 onions, chopped
- 4 cloves garlic, minced
- 4 teaspoons white sugar
- 1/4 cup chopped fresh basil
- salt to taste
- ground black pepper to taste
- 2 pinches baking soda
- 1/4 cup grated Parmesan cheese

Direction

- Mix together whole tomatoes, tomato sauce, tomato paste, water, mushrooms, onions, garlic, sugar, salt and pepper,

basil, and 1 pinch of baking soda in a large saucepan. Bring to a boil, stirring. Reduce to a simmer, and cook for 4 hours minimum.
- Stir in another pinch of baking soda; the sauce will foam. Simmer, stirring occasionally, until thick and almost brown. Make sure to scrape the sides of the pan in to the sauce.
- After the sauce is fork consistency, stir in Parmesan cheese. Watch that the cheese does not burn. Taste sauce. If it is too tangy or acidic, add another pinch of baking soda and simmer another 1/2 hour.
- Cool, cover, and refrigerate overnight. The next day, reheat and serve.

Nutrition Information

- Calories: 169 calories
- Total Fat: 1.7 g
- Cholesterol: 2 mg
- Sodium: 1624 mg
- Total Carbohydrate: 36.3 g
- Protein: 9.1 g

Nannys Spaghetti Sauce

"This is my Sicilian great-grandmother's recipe. I've never tasted better. Serve with meatballs and Italian sausage; it's also terrific as a marinara sauce."

SERVING: 6

Ingredients

- 1 (28 ounce) can crushed tomatoes
- 2 (8 ounce) cans tomato sauce
- 1 (6 ounce) can tomato paste
- 3 cloves garlic, minced
- 1 tablespoon white sugar
- 2 tablespoons red wine vinegar
- 2 teaspoons dried oregano
- 1 pinch crushed red pepper flakes

Direction

- In a large skillet combine the crushed tomatoes, tomato paste, tomato sauce, garlic, sugar, vinegar, oregano and red pepper flakes. Stir all together and simmer over low heat for at least 30 minutes (for the best flavor). Stir frequently to prevent burning.

Nutrition Information

- Calories: 97 calories

- Total Fat: 0.7 g
- Cholesterol: 0 mg
- Sodium: 788 mg
- Total Carbohydrate: 22.3 g
- Protein: 4.5 g

Pasta Primavera Sauce

"This pasta sauce is low-fat but doesn't taste it!"

SERVING: 6

Ingredients

- 1 (14.5 ounce) can diced tomatoes
- 1 (6 ounce) can tomato paste
- 3/4 cup fresh broccoli florets
- 3/4 cup thinly sliced carrots
- 3/4 cup sliced onion
- 1/2 cup zucchini chunks
- 1/2 cup sliced green bell pepper
- 1/2 cup red bell pepper, sliced
- 2 cloves garlic, chopped
- 2 bay leaf
- 1 tablespoon olive oil
- 1/2 teaspoon dried basil
- 1/2 teaspoon dried rosemary
- 1/2 teaspoon dried oregano
- 1/2 teaspoon dried thyme
- 1 1/2 teaspoons salt
- 1/4 teaspoon ground black pepper
- 1 teaspoon white sugar
- 1/2 cup water

Direction

- In a large pot combine tomatoes, tomato paste, broccoli, carrots, onion, zucchini, green bell pepper, red bell pepper, garlic, bay leaves, olive oil, basil, rosemary, oregano, thyme, salt, pepper, sugar, and water. Heat to just boiling, cover and reduce heat to simmer. Cook until all vegetable are tender, approximately 45 minutes. Stir occasionally.

Nutrition Information

- Calories: 84 calories
- Total Fat: 2.6 g
- Cholesterol: 0 mg
- Sodium: 975 mg
- Total Carbohydrate: 13.8 g
- Protein: 2.8 g

Pasta Sauce Vegan

"Vegetable-loaded tomato-based pasta sauce for vegans."

SERVING: 6 | PREP: 35 M | COOK: 1 H 20 M | READY IN: 1 H 55 M

Ingredients

- 1/4 cup chopped celery
- 1/4 cup chopped green bell pepper
- 1/4 cup chopped red bell pepper
- 1/4 cup chopped yellow bell pepper
- 1/4 cup chopped carrot
- 2 tablespoons basil, or to taste
- 2 tablespoons oregano, or to taste
- 1/4 teaspoon thyme, or to taste
- 1 tablespoon salt, or to taste
- 1 tablespoon ground black pepper, or to taste
- 3 tablespoons olive oil
- 1/4 cup chopped white onion
- 4 cloves garlic, minced
- 20 ripe tomatoes - peeled, seeded, and chopped
- 1/2 cup red wine, divided
- 2 tablespoons cornstarch

Direction

- Mix celery, green bell pepper, red bell pepper, yellow bell pepper, carrot, basil, oregano, thyme, salt, and black pepper

together in a bowl until the vegetables are evenly coated in seasonings.
- Heat olive oil in a skillet over medium-low heat. Cook and stir onion and garlic in hot oil until onion is soft and garlic is light golden brown, 5 to 10 minutes. Add vegetable mixture to the skillet; cook and stir until hot, 3 to 5 minutes. Remove skillet from heat.
- Combine tomatoes and 1/4 cup red wine in a large pot over low heat. Cook, stirring occasionally, until the tomatoes begin to soften, 15 to 20 minutes.
- Pour tomato mixture into a blender with remaining 1/4 cup red wine and cornstarch to no more than half full. Cover and hold lid down; pulse a few times before leaving on to blend. Puree in batches until smooth.
- Return blended tomatoes to pot over medium-low heat. Stir vegetable mixture through tomato sauce; bring to a simmer and cook until thick, about 1 hour.

Nutrition Information

- Calories: 500 calories
- Total Fat: 20.3 g
- Cholesterol: 0 mg
- Sodium: 3419 mg
- Total Carbohydrate: 72.4 g
- Protein: 10.7 g

Pasta With Roasted Eggplant Sauce

"If you like eggplant, you should try this! The sauce for this pasta is made by roasting eggplant and garlic in the oven, then making a paste from it after it's soft. Make sure you find the perfect eggplant, otherwise it could leave you with a bitter recipe. It turned out great for me!"

SERVING: 4 | PREP: 15 M | COOK: 30 M | READY IN: 45 M

Ingredients

- 2 small eggplants, peeled and cut into 1-inch cubes
- 6 cloves garlic, crushed and peeled
- 1/2 cup extra-virgin olive oil
- salt and ground black pepper to taste
- 1 (16 ounce) package penne pasta
- 2 tablespoons extra-virgin olive oil
- 1 yellow onion, finely chopped
- 1 (28 ounce) can diced tomatoes
- 1 cup fresh basil leaves

Direction

- Preheat oven to 400 degrees F (200 degrees C).
- Spread eggplants and garlic cloves on a rimmed baking sheet. Brush with 1/2 cup olive oil; season with salt and pepper.
- Roast in the preheated oven until soft, about 20 minutes.
- Bring a large pot of lightly salted water to a boil while eggplants and garlic are roasting. Add penne and cook,

stirring occasionally, until tender yet firm to the bite, about 11 minutes. Drain.
- Heat 2 tablespoons oil in a large skillet over medium heat. Add onion; cook and stir until softened, about 5 minutes.
- Place eggplants and garlic in a food processor; process into a smooth paste. Stir paste into the onions in the skillet. Stir in tomatoes. Cook until heated through, about 5 minutes. Season sauce with salt and pepper. Toss hot penne and basil into the sauce and mix together.

Nutrition Information

- Calories: 827 calories
- Total Fat: 37.8 g
- Cholesterol: 0 mg
- Sodium: 359 mg
- Total Carbohydrate: 104.8 g
- Protein: 19.5 g

Pastapizza Sauce

"My mom gave me this recipe. It's a very quick and versatile sauce that may be doubled or tripled. Substitute other cheeses and herbs for variety."

SERVING: 2 | PREP: 2 M | COOK: 13 M | READY IN: 15 M

Ingredients

- 2 tablespoons olive oil
- 2 cloves garlic, chopped
- 1 (6 ounce) can tomato paste
- 2 teaspoons white sugar
- 1/4 teaspoon dried oregano
- 1/4 teaspoon dried basil
- 2/3 cup water
- 2 tablespoons grated Parmesan cheese
- 2 tablespoons red wine
- salt and pepper to taste

Direction

- In large skillet, sauté garlic in oil until golden. Add tomato paste, sugar, oregano, basil, water, cheese and wine. Season with salt and pepper and simmer 10 minutes over medium-low heat.

Nutrition Information

- Calories: 245 calories
- Total Fat: 15.4 g
- Cholesterol: 4 mg
- Sodium: 749 mg
- Total Carbohydrate: 22 g
- Protein: 5.8 g

Peanut Sauce Ii

"Gingery and slightly spicy, this is my family's favorite peanut sauce."

SERVING: 8 | PREP: 25 M | COOK: 5 M | READY IN: 30 M

Ingredients

- 1/4 cup vegetable oil
- 1 cup chopped onion
- 2 cloves garlic, minced
- 2 tablespoons minced fresh ginger root
- 1 jalapeno pepper, seeded and minced
- 1 cup peanut butter
- 1 1/4 cups water
- 1/4 cup tamari or soy sauce
- 3 tablespoons honey
- 1/4 cup fresh basil leaves, cut into thin strips
- 3 fresh basil leaves for garnish (optional)

Direction

- Heat the vegetable oil in a skillet over medium heat. Stir in onion; cook and stir until the onion has softened and turned translucent, about 5 minutes. Add garlic, jalapeno pepper, and ginger; cook and stir for 2 minutes more.
- Stir in peanut butter, water, tamari, and honey until smooth. Add shredded basil. Heat through, and remove from heat. Garnish with whole basil leaves, if desired.

Nutrition Information

- Calories: 290 calories
- Total Fat: 23.1 g
- Cholesterol: 0 mg
- Sodium: 649 mg
- Total Carbohydrate: 15.8 g
- Protein: 9.4 g

Penne With Vegan Arrabbiata Sauce

"This is a nice dish, meatless and goes well with a small side salad, piece of bread and a hearty appetite."

SERVING: 14 | PREP: 15 M | COOK: 3 H | READY IN: 3 H 20 M

Ingredients

- 1 pound penne pasta
- 1 cup extra virgin olive oil
- 7 cloves garlic, minced
- 7 (28 ounce) cans crushed tomatoes
- 2 1/2 teaspoons crushed red pepper flakes
- 2 bay leaves
- 10 leaves fresh basil

Direction

- Bring a large pot of lightly salted water to a boil. Add pasta and cook for 8 to 10 minutes or until al dente; drain.
- Heat olive oil, and cook garlic just until softened. Add remaining ingredients. Simmer over low heat and cook at least 3 hours.
- Add cooked penne pasta and let sit at least 5 minutes before stirring and serving.

Nutrition Information

- Calories: 389 calories
- Total Fat: 17.9 g
- Cholesterol: 0 mg

- Sodium: 519 mg
- Total Carbohydrate: 52.9 g
- Protein: 10.9 g

Pepper And Olive Pasta Sauce

"This dish is different than the typical red sauce pasta dish. It's light, but not wimpy. You can use any color of pepper in this sauce."

SERVING: 4 | PREP: 20 M | COOK: 40 M | READY IN: 1 H

Ingredients

- 1/2 cup olive oil
- 4 cloves garlic, minced
- 5 green bell peppers, cut into 1/4 inch strips
- 8 ounces kalamata olives
- 1/2 teaspoon crushed red pepper
- 1 cup white wine
- 32 ounces tomato-vegetable juice cocktail
- 1 teaspoon dried basil leaves
- 1/2 teaspoon dried oregano
- 1 pinch white sugar
- salt and pepper to taste
- 1 tablespoon chopped fresh parsley

Direction

- In a large skillet, heat the oil on high and add the garlic. Reduce to medium high and cook until the garlic begins to turn golden, then add the peppers. Cook until the peppers

are soft and turning brown around the edges. Add the olives and crushed red pepper and stir. Pour in the wine and cook for 2 minutes.
- Add the tomato-vegetable juice cocktail, basil, oregano, sugar, salt and pepper. Bring to a boil and reduce heat to medium. Cook until liquid is halved. Stir in parsley. Serve over your favorite pasta.

Nutrition Information

- Calories: 541 calories
- Total Fat: 42.2 g
- Cholesterol: 0 mg
- Sodium: 1843 mg
- Total Carbohydrate: 27 g
- Protein: 4.5 g

Pesto Del Sol

"After they baste in the sun all summer long, I cut down my basil plants and make this delightful pesto. This basil pesto has been mellowed with fresh spinach and enhanced by the taste of black olives. I make big batches and freeze in small container for the whole year. It will keep in the fridge for a week. Toss with pasta. Spread on meat or sandwiches. Add a spoonful for favoring to lots of recipes. Enjoy!"

SERVING: 12 | PREP: 20 M | READY IN: 20 M

Ingredients

- 1 cup packed fresh spinach
- 1 cup packed fresh basil
- 3/4 cup pine nuts
- 1/2 cup walnuts
- 24 small black olives
- 4 cloves garlic
- 1 cup grated Parmesan cheese
- 1/2 cup grated Romano cheese
- 1 cup olive oil
- 1 dash black pepper

Direction

- In a food processor, blend spinach, basil, pine nuts, walnuts, olives and garlic. Blend in Parmesan cheese and Romano cheese. Gradually add oil, processing until smooth; season with pepper. Serve at room temperature.

Nutrition Information

- Calories: 298 calories
- Total Fat: 29.5 g
- Cholesterol: 11 mg
- Sodium: 220 mg
- Total Carbohydrate: 3.3 g
- Protein: 7.3 g

Pesto With Arugula

"This pesto is unique due to the arugula, which gives it a peppery bite. I also like the lack of cheese, but add it if you must. Use as a spread or on pasta. My favorite is on baguette slices or on whole wheat crackers. It's addictive!"

SERVING: 12 | PREP: 15 M | READY IN: 15 M

Ingredients

- 1 1/2 cups baby arugula leaves
- 1 1/2 cups fresh basil leaves
- 2/3 cup pine nuts
- 8 cloves garlic
- 1 (6 ounce) can black olives, drained
- 3/4 cup extra virgin olive oil
- 1/2 lime, juiced
- 1 teaspoon red wine vinegar
- 1/8 teaspoon ground cumin
- 1 pinch ground cayenne pepper
- salt and pepper to taste

Direction

- Place the arugula, basil, pine nuts, garlic, and olives in a food processor, and chop to a coarse paste. Mix in olive oil, lime juice, vinegar, cumin, cayenne pepper, salt, and pepper. Process until well blended and smooth.

Nutrition Information

- Calories: 191 calories
- Total Fat: 19.4 g
- Cholesterol: 0 mg
- Sodium: 125 mg
- Total Carbohydrate: 3.2 g
- Protein: 2.3 g

Pomodoro Pasta Sauce

"A smooth, tasty tomato-based sauce full of fresh ingredients! Great as a pasta sauce or dipping sauce for garlic bread! Super kid-friendly!"

SERVING: 16 | PREP: 20 M | COOK: 1 H | READY IN: 1 H 20 M

Ingredients

- 1 (28 ounce) can diced tomatoes
- 2 stalks celery, with leaves, chopped
- 2 carrots, peeled and chopped
- 1 small sweet onion, chopped
- 3 cloves garlic
- 1/2 (6 ounce) can tomato paste
- 2 cups water
- 2 cups red wine
- 1 teaspoon dried sage
- 1 teaspoon dried basil
- 1 teaspoon dried parsley
- 1 tablespoon dried oregano
- salt and ground black pepper to taste

Direction

- Stir the diced tomatoes, celery, carrots, sweet onion, garlic, tomato paste, water, red wine, sage, basil, parsley, oregano, salt, and pepper together in a large pot and bring to a boil. Reduce heat to low and cook the sauce at a simmer until the carrots are tender, about 1 hour.

- Pour the sauce into a blender, filling the pitcher no more than halfway. Hold the lid of the blender in place with a towel and carefully start the blender using a few quick pulses to get the sauce moving before leaving it on to puree. Puree in batches until smooth and pour into a clean container. Alternately, you can use a stick blender and puree the sauce in the pot.

Nutrition Information

- Calories: 48 calories
- Total Fat: 0.1 g
- Cholesterol: 0 mg
- Sodium: 131 mg
- Total Carbohydrate: 5.3 g
- Protein: 0.9 g

Portobello Mushroom Bolognese Sauce

"This is a vegetarian option I created for Bolognese sauce - and it could fool the unsuspecting! Serve over pasta with Parmesan cheese. Enjoy!"

SERVING: 4 | PREP: 15 M | COOK: 3 H 22 M | READY IN: 3 H 37 M

Ingredients

- 1 onion, quartered
- 1 large stalk celery, halved
- 1 carrot, quartered
- 4 large portobello mushrooms, stemmed
- 1 tablespoon vegetable oil, or to taste
- salt to taste
- 1/2 cup white wine
- 1/4 cup milk
- 1/4 teaspoon ground nutmeg
- 2 (15 ounce) cans whole tomatoes, or more to taste
- 1/2 cup water (optional)

Direction

- Pulse onion in a food processor until diced but not mushy. Transfer to a bowl. Repeat with celery and carrot. Pulse portobello mushrooms to the consistency of ground beef.
- Coat the bottom of a large pot with oil; heat over low heat. Cook and stir onion in the oil until soft but not browned,

about 5 minutes. Stir in celery and carrot; cook until slightly softened, about 5 minutes. Add portobello mushrooms; cook about 1 minute. Season with salt.
- Pour wine into the pot. Increase heat to medium-high; stir with a flat wooden spoon until bottom of the pot looks almost dry, 3 to 5 minutes. Add milk and nutmeg. Reduce heat to medium; cook and stir until bottom of the pot is almost dry, 3 to 5 minutes.
- Pour tomato juice from the cans into the pot. Pulse tomatoes in the food processor until coarsely chopped; stir into the pot. Bring to a boil; reduce heat to low and simmer until flavors combine, 3 to 4 hours. Thin sauce with water if it appears too thick.

Nutrition Information

- Calories: 128 calories
- Total Fat: 4.1 g
- Cholesterol: 1 mg
- Sodium: 368 mg
- Total Carbohydrate: 16.5 g
- Protein: 3 g

Presto Vegan Pesto

"Honestly, I really never liked pesto. However, now that I am tasting things so clearly (as a vegan), I LOVE the stuff! Here's my new, favorite Presto Pesto!"

SERVING: 4 | PREP: 5 M | READY IN: 5 M

Ingredients

- 1 bunch fresh basil
- 1/3 cup pine nuts
- 5 cloves garlic
- 1/2 cup olive oil
- 1 tablespoon lemon juice
- 2 tablespoons water
- 1/4 cup Parmesan flavor grated soy topping

Direction

- Place the basil, pine nuts, garlic, olive oil, lemon juice, water, and soy topping into a blender. Cover, and puree until smooth.

Nutrition Information

- Calories: 337 calories
- Total Fat: 32.9 g
- Cholesterol: 0 mg
- Sodium: 100 mg
- Total Carbohydrate: 5.2 g
- Protein: 6.6 g

Proper Pesto

"There are lots of recipes people claim taste better if made by hand, but there's no easier case to prove that than pesto. The intensity of the flavors is beyond compare, and as if by some kind of magic, this gorgeous spread develops an addictive spiciness. You can taste each ingredient, and yet when smashed together, new and wonderful flavors are released."

SERVING: 8 | PREP: 10 M | READY IN: 35 M

Ingredients

- 4 cloves garlic, peeled
- 1/4 teaspoon kosher salt
- 1 large bunch fresh basil
- 3 tablespoons pine nuts
- 2 ounces finely grated Parmigiano-Reggiano cheese
- 1/2 cup mild extra-virgin olive oil

Direction

- Crush garlic and pinch of kosher salt in a mortar with the pestle until garlic is mashed and paste-like, 1 or 2 minutes. Add basil in 3 or 4 additions, crushing and pounding down the leaves until they form a fairly fine paste, about 8 minutes or more depending on size of leaves and thickness of stems. Add and pound in pine nuts.
- Transfer a handful of grated cheese to mortar and pound into the sauce. Add another handful of cheese and incorporate into the mixture. Continue adding cheese a

handful at a time until completely incorporated, about 5 minutes.
- Drizzle in olive oil 1 tablespoon at a time, pounding it into the sauce. When all the olive oil has been added and emulsified into the mixture, transfer pesto to a bowl and drizzle surface with olive oil.

Nutrition Information

- Calories: 181 calories
- Total Fat: 17.8 g
- Cholesterol: 6 mg
- Sodium: 169 mg
- Total Carbohydrate: 1.7 g
- Protein: 4.1 g

Puttanesca Ii

"A good friend gave me this recipe and I've since found it to be so tasty and best of all, easy! My family loves it and it doesn't take long to make at all! It's perfect over angel hair pasta with garlic bread on the side! Double the recipe for larger parties or just for leftovers!"

SERVING: 4 | PREP: 15 M | COOK: 30 M | READY IN: 45 M

Ingredients

- 1 teaspoon olive oil
- 1 teaspoon butter
- 1 large onion, finely chopped
- 1 clove garlic, minced
- 1 (8 ounce) can crushed tomatoes
- 1 (8 ounce) can diced tomatoes
- 1 cup sun-dried tomatoes
- 1/2 cup hot cherry peppers
- 1/2 cup sliced black olives
- 1/2 cup sliced green olives
- 1/2 teaspoon capers

Direction

- Heat oil and butter in a large saucepan over medium heat. Sauté onion and garlic until onion is tender and translucent. Stir in crushed tomatoes, diced tomatoes and sun-dried tomatoes. Simmer 5 minutes on medium heat. Add peppers, black olives, green olives and capers. Simmer 15 to 20 minutes on low heat, or until sauce has thickened.

Nutrition Information

- Calories: 152 calories
- Total Fat: 7 g
- Cholesterol: 3 mg
- Sodium: 1190 mg
- Total Carbohydrate: 20.9 g
- Protein: 4.3 g

Quick Pasta Sauce

"This is a quick and easy recipe. "

SERVING: 6 | PREP: 5 M | COOK: 25 M | READY IN: 30 M

Ingredients

- 2 tablespoons olive oil
- 3 cloves garlic, minced
- 1 teaspoon dried basil
- 1 (28 ounce) can crushed tomatoes
- salt and pepper to taste

Direction

- In a large skillet over medium heat, sauté garlic in oil until tender, 2 minutes. Stir in basil and crushed tomatoes. Season with salt and pepper and cook 15 to 20 minutes, until slightly thickened. Serve immediately.

Nutrition Information

- Calories: 84 calories
- Total Fat: 4.9 g
- Cholesterol: 0 mg
- Sodium: 173 mg
- Total Carbohydrate: 10.2 g
- Protein: 2.3 g

Roasted Tomato Sauce

"Roma tomatoes and garlic are oven roasted and caramelized to give your pasta a deep, rich flavor. Roasting the tomatoes really draws out the sweet flavor, which mixes so well with the roasted garlic."

SERVING: 2 | PREP: 10 M | COOK: 35 M | READY IN: 50 M

Ingredients

- 1 pound roma (plum) tomatoes, halved and seeded
- 2 cloves garlic, peeled
- 1 tablespoon olive oil
- 1 pinch salt and freshly ground black pepper to taste
- 10 leaves basil, torn

Direction

- Preheat the oven to 375 degrees F (190 degrees C). Line a baking sheet with parchment paper or aluminum foil.
- Place tomato halves skin-side down on the prepared baking sheet. Add garlic cloves. Evenly drizzle tomatoes and garlic with olive oil and season with salt and pepper.
- Roast in the preheated oven until tomatoes are bubbling, about 25 minutes. Increase heat to 425 degrees F (220 degrees C). Roast until tomatoes just begin to brown, 10 more minutes. Turn off the heat. Let tomatoes sit in the hot oven with the door closed until further caramelized, about 5 minutes.
- Transfer roasted tomatoes and garlic to a bowl. Add basil and use a wooden spoon to crush the mixture and break

apart the tomatoes, leaving them a bit chunky. Remove peels, if desired. Serve over your favorite cooked pasta.

Nutrition Information

- Calories: 106 calories
- Total Fat: 7.2 g
- Cholesterol: 0 mg
- Sodium: 90 mg
- Total Carbohydrate: 10 g
- Protein: 2.3 g

Salsa Di Noci

"A local chef in Cinque Terre prepared this dish for us using the herbs we'd picked only moments before. 15 years after trying the dish for the first time, we still make it at home often."

SERVING: 4 | PREP: 10 M | COOK: 15 M | READY IN: 25 M

Ingredients

- 3 cups water, or as needed
- 1 1/2 cups walnuts
- 2 cloves garlic, peeled
- 1 pinch sea salt
- 1 teaspoon chopped fresh marjoram
- 1 teaspoon chopped fresh thyme
- 1 teaspoon chopped fresh oregano
- 1/2 cup extra-virgin olive oil
- 3/4 cup heavy cream
- 1 cup finely grated Pecorino Romano cheese
- freshly ground black pepper to taste
- sea salt to taste
- 1 (16 ounce) box dry fettuccine pasta
- 1/2 bunch fresh chives, finely chopped

Direction

- Bring water to a boil in a small saucepan. Add walnuts and cook until they have softened slightly, about 5 minutes. Drain and set aside.
- Combine garlic and 1 pinch sea salt in the bowl of a mortar and pestle. Grind to create a thick paste. Add walnuts,

- marjoram, thyme, and oregano. Grind until combined and slightly creamy, but still coarse.
- Transfer the walnut mixture to a large bowl. Slowly whisk in olive oil to form a thick emulsion. Add heavy cream and Pecorino Romano cheese, whisk until combined. Season with black pepper and sea salt to taste.
- Fill a large pot with lightly salted water and bring to a rolling boil. Stir in the fettuccine, return to a boil, and cook pasta over medium heat until cooked through but still firm to the bite, about 8 minutes. Drain.
- Toss walnut sauce with pasta. Garnish with fresh chives.

Nutrition Information

- Calories: 1116 calories
- Total Fat: 74.7 g
- Cholesterol: 71 mg
- Sodium: 370 mg
- Total Carbohydrate: 90.4 g
- Protein: 26.3 g

Seven Ingredient Tomato Sauce

"This is a very simple recipe to make and tastes great too. This sauce tastes extra good if you add fried meatballs or pork spareribs to the sauce. Another good addition is a can of drained peas, if you like them. Happy eating!"

SERVING: 14 | PREP: 10 M | COOK: 3 H | READY IN: 3 H 10 M

Ingredients

- 2 tablespoons olive oil
- 7 cloves garlic, minced
- 1 (6 ounce) can tomato paste
- 1 (28 ounce) can crushed tomatoes
- 2 (28 ounce) cans tomato puree
- 1/2 teaspoon ground black pepper
- 1/2 teaspoon salt
- 2 teaspoons dried basil leaves
- 1 teaspoon white sugar

Direction

- Heat the olive oil in a large saucepan and cook and stir garlic, being careful not to burn it. Pour in tomato paste and simmer on low for 5 minutes. Add crushed tomatoes, tomato puree, pepper, salt, basil and sugar; stir. Cook on low for three hours, stirring occasionally.

Nutrition Information

- Calories: 91 calories
- Total Fat: 2.4 g
- Cholesterol: 0 mg
- Sodium: 700 mg
- Total Carbohydrate: 17.3 g
- Protein: 3.4 g

Sicilian Lentil Pasta Sauce

"This is a very nice, thick sauce. It has a meat taste, without the meat. Nice and hearty, great with a crusty bread on a cold, Fall day."

SERVING: 8 | PREP: 20 M | COOK: 1 H 20 M | READY IN: 1 H 40 M

Ingredients

- 2 teaspoons olive oil
- 1 cup chopped onion
- 2 cups fresh sliced mushrooms
- 1 small zucchini, chopped
- 3 cloves garlic, minced
- 1 cup dry lentils
- 3 cups water
- 2 (8 ounce) cans tomato sauce
- 1 (6 ounce) can tomato paste
- 1 1/2 teaspoons white sugar
- 1/2 cup water

Direction

- In a large saucepan, heat oil over medium heat. Add onions, mushrooms, zucchini, and garlic. Cook and stir until tender, about 5 minutes.
- Add lentils and 3 cups water to vegetables. Bring to a rolling boil, stirring occasionally. Reduce heat to low, cover, and cook 45 to 60 minutes.

- Stir in tomato sauce, tomato paste, sugar, and 1/2 cup water. Bring to a boil. Reduce heat, cover, and simmer for 20 minutes. If necessary, add more water to keep the sauce from sticking. Be careful not to dilute; the sauce should be quite thick.

Nutrition Information

- Calories: 145 calories
- Total Fat: 1.8 g
- Cholesterol: 0 mg
- Sodium: 466 mg
- Total Carbohydrate: 25.5 g
- Protein: 8.9 g

Simple Arrabbiata Sauce

"Simple and spicy, with an incredible flavor."

SERVING: 4 | PREP: 5 M | COOK: 40 M | READY IN: 45 M

Ingredients

- 2 (28 ounce) cans diced tomatoes
- 2 tablespoons olive oil
- 1 teaspoon crushed red pepper flakes
- 4 cloves garlic, minced
- 1/3 cup chopped fresh basil
- 1/2 teaspoon salt and pepper to taste

Direction

- In a large saucepan, combine tomatoes, olive oil, and red pepper flakes. Simmer 30 to 40 minutes, or until sauce is thickened. Stir in garlic, and simmer 10 minutes. Remove from heat, and stir in basil, salt and pepper.

Nutrition Information

- Calories: 148 calories
- Total Fat: 6.9 g
- Cholesterol: 0 mg
- Sodium: 907 mg
- Total Carbohydrate: 14.5 g
- Protein: 3.6 g

Simple Garlic And Basil Pesto

"This recipe is something that you can make quickly and easily using a blender. Everything you need is easy to find in your local supermarket. This paste is great for putting on or in meat and pastas, or with cottage cheese in stuffed pasta shells. Once I start making this, the orders from friends and family keep coming in. For best taste, pesto should be heated up in the meal it's being prepared with."

SERVING: 12 | PREP: 15 M | READY IN: 15 M

Ingredients

- 3 cups chopped fresh basil
- 1 cup extra virgin olive oil
- 1/2 cup pine nuts
- 1/8 cup Brazil nuts
- 2/3 cup grated Parmesan cheese
- 2 tablespoons minced garlic
- 1/2 teaspoon chili powder

Direction

- Place the basil in a blender. Pour in about 1 tablespoon of the oil, and blend basil into a paste. Gradually add pine nuts, Brazil nuts, Parmesan cheese, garlic, chili powder, and remaining oil. Continue to blend until smooth.

Nutrition Information

- Calories: 234 calories

- Total Fat: 23.9 g
- Cholesterol: 4 mg
- Sodium: 70 mg
- Total Carbohydrate: 1.9 g
- Protein: 3.7 g

Slow Cooker Spaghetti Sauce I

"This sauce recipe has been handed down from generation to generation. It's a family favorite and left-over sauce freezes well. Best when cooked all day in a slow cooker. Since there is no added oil this sauce is fat free."

SERVING: 10 | PREP: 10 M | COOK: 4 H | READY IN: 4 H 10 M

Ingredients

- 5 (29 ounce) cans tomato sauce
- 3 (6 ounce) cans tomato paste
- 3 cloves garlic, minced
- 1 onion, chopped
- 3 tablespoons dried rosemary
- 3 tablespoons dried oregano
- 3 tablespoons dried thyme
- 3 tablespoons dried parsley
- 1 bay leaf
- 1 pinch crushed red pepper flakes

Direction

- In a large slow cooker combine tomato sauce, tomato paste, garlic, onion, rosemary, oregano, thyme, parsley, bay leaf and red pepper. Cook on high for 3 to 4 hours, stir frequently.

Nutrition Information

- Calories: 157 calories

- Total Fat: 1.4 g
- Cholesterol: 0 mg
- Sodium: 2534 mg
- Total Carbohydrate: 35.4 g
- Protein: 8.2 g

Spaghetti Sauce Ii

"A very thick and dark sauce with a little red pepper kick. Adjust the crushed red pepper to suit your tastes. This sauce freezes well too."

SERVING: 6

Ingredients

- 1 onion, chopped
- 3 cloves garlic, minced
- 2 tablespoons olive oil
- 1 (28 ounce) can whole peeled tomatoes
- 2 (6 ounce) cans tomato paste
- 2 tablespoons dried basil
- 1 tablespoon dried oregano
- 2 bay leaves
- 1 tablespoon white sugar
- 1/4 teaspoon crushed red pepper flakes
- 1/4 cup red wine
- 1 pound Italian sausage links (optional)

Direction

- Heat olive oil in a large saucepan or Dutch oven. Sauté onions and garlic until tender, 2-3 minutes. Add remaining ingredients (except sausage links) and simmer over low heat for 3 hours.
- With one hour cooking time remaining, cook and brown sausages in a skillet. When browned, place in sauce and

continue to simmer. Remove bay leaves before serving. Serve over hot cooked noodles, with sausages on the side.

Nutrition Information

- Calories: 403 calories
- Total Fat: 28.8 g
- Cholesterol: 58 mg
- Sodium: 1190 mg
- Total Carbohydrate: 22.5 g
- Protein: 14.9 g

Spaghetti Sauce With Cauliflower

"Serve this sauce over your favorite pasta. This recipe goes back to the Great Depression. My large Italian family gathered in the kitchen and tried many ways to prepare Sunday dinner on a tight budget. My friends and family couldn't believe that there is no ground beef in this sauce. I bring it into work the next day and share. Co-workers love it."

SERVING: 8 | PREP: 20 M | COOK: 1 H | READY IN: 1 H 20 M

Ingredients

- 1/4 cup olive oil
- 6 large cloves garlic, chopped
- 1 sweet onion (such as Vidalia®), chopped
- 3 cups chopped cauliflower
- 1 teaspoon dried basil
- 1/2 teaspoon black pepper
- 3 (28 ounce) cans crushed tomatoes

Direction

- Heat the olive oil over medium heat in a large saucepan or soup pot, and cook the garlic, onion, and cauliflower, stirring occasionally, until the cauliflower is browned and tender, about 30 minutes. Pour in the basil, black pepper, and crushed tomatoes, and simmer until the sauce is thickened and the flavors have blended, about 30 more minutes.

Nutrition Information

- Calories: 177 calories
- Total Fat: 7.7 g
- Cholesterol: 0 mg
- Sodium: 401 mg
- Total Carbohydrate: 26.6 g
- Protein: 6 g

Spaghetti Sauce With Fresh Tomatoes

"Made with fresh tomatoes! Wonderful taste. Serve over spaghetti noodles and add grated Parmesan cheese as desired."

SERVING: 8 | PREP: 15 M | COOK: 1 H 10 M | READY IN: 1 H 25 M

Ingredients

- 1/4 cup olive oil
- 1 onion, chopped
- 1/2 teaspoon garlic powder
- 4 pounds fresh tomatoes, peeled and chopped
- 1 tablespoon white sugar
- 1 tablespoon dried basil
- 1 tablespoon dried parsley
- 1 teaspoon salt

Direction

- Heat olive oil in a large skillet over medium heat. Add onion and garlic powder; cook and stir until onion is translucent, about 5 minutes. Add tomatoes, sugar, basil, parsley, and salt. Bring to a boil. Reduce heat and simmer, stirring occasionally, until sauce thickens, 1 to 2 hours.

Nutrition Information

- Calories: 120 calories
- Total Fat: 7.3 g
- Cholesterol: 0 mg

- Sodium: 304 mg
- Total Carbohydrate: 13.5 g
- Protein: 2.5 g

Sugo Di Pomodoro Authentic Italian Tomato Sauce

"This is a basic recipe for authentic Italian tomato sauce flavored with extra-virgin olive oil, garlic and basil. Toss with your favorite pasta or use for pizza, gnocchi and more."

SERVING: 4 | PREP: 5 M | COOK: 25 M | READY IN: 30 M

Ingredients

- 2 tablespoons extra-virgin olive oil
- 1 onion, chopped
- 4 cloves garlic, halved
- 2 (14 ounce) cans passata (crushed tomatoes)
- 1/4 cup fresh basil, torn in half
- salt to taste

Direction

- Heat oil in a saucepan over low heat. Add onion and garlic. Cook and stir until soft and translucent, about 5 minutes. Add passata, basil, and salt. Cover and simmer over medium heat, stirring occasionally, until tomato sauce has thickened, about 20 minutes. Remove garlic halves before serving.

Nutrition Information

- Calories: 152 calories
- Total Fat: 7.4 g
- Cholesterol: 0 mg
- Sodium: 304 mg
- Total Carbohydrate: 20.8 g
- Protein: 4.2 g

Sundried Tomato Pesto

"The best sun-dried tomato pesto."

SERVING: 40 | PREP: 20 M | READY IN: 20 M

Ingredients

- 4 ounces sun-dried tomatoes
- 2 tablespoons chopped fresh basil
- 2 tablespoons chopped fresh parsley
- 1 tablespoon chopped garlic
- 1/4 cup chopped pine nuts
- 3 tablespoons chopped onion
- 1/4 cup balsamic vinegar
- 1 tablespoon tomato paste
- 1/3 cup crushed tomatoes
- 1/4 cup red wine
- 1/2 cup olive oil
- 1/2 cup grated Parmesan cheese
- salt to taste

Direction

- Place sun-dried tomatoes in a bowl and cover with warm water for 5 minutes, or until tender.
- In a food processor or blender combine sun-dried tomatoes, basil, parsley, garlic, pine nuts and onion; process until well blended. Add vinegar, tomato paste, crushed tomatoes and red wine, and process. Stir in olive oil and Parmesan cheese. Season with salt to taste.

Nutrition Information

- Calories: 44 calories
- Total Fat: 3.5 g
- Cholesterol: < 1 mg
- Sodium: 81 mg
- Total Carbohydrate: 2.4 g
- Protein: 1.1 g

Tamras Lemon Artichoke Pesto

"Chopped artichoke hearts with garlic, lemon juice, and Parmesan. Great on rotelle pasta or as an appetizer on mini toasts. Tastes just like the stuff I was paying too much for at the specialty market. We freeze the leftovers in an ice tray for easy weekday dinners."

SERVING: 8 | PREP: 15 M | READY IN: 15 M

Ingredients

- 1/4 cup chopped fresh cilantro
- 8 medium garlic cloves
- 4 tablespoons lemon juice
- 1/2 teaspoon cayenne pepper
- 1 cup walnuts
- 1/2 cup canola oil
- 1/2 cup olive oil
- salt to taste
- 1 (8 ounce) package frozen artichokes, thawed and chopped
- 1/2 cup grated Parmesan cheese

Direction

- Place the cilantro, garlic, lemon juice, cayenne pepper, walnuts, canola oil, olive oil, and salt into a food processor. Pulse until smooth, then pour into a large bowl. Gently stir in chopped artichokes and Parmesan cheese.

Nutrition Information

- Calories: 386 calories
- Total Fat: 39.2 g
- Cholesterol: 6 mg
- Sodium: 111 mg
- Total Carbohydrate: 6.2 g
- Protein: 5.7 g

The Very Best Spaghetti Sauce

"This is sooooo good! It's a slow cooked, meatless spaghetti sauce with TONS and TONS of vegetables, and its just sooooo good! Enjoy!"

SERVING: 12 | PREP: 30 M | COOK: 6 H 30 M | READY IN: 7 H

Ingredients

- 18 roma (plum) tomatoes
- 2 (6 ounce) cans tomato paste
- 1/2 cup butter
- 4 cloves garlic, minced
- 5 bay leaves
- 1 large white onion, chopped
- 1 large zucchini, chopped
- 1 green bell pepper, chopped
- 1 red bell pepper, chopped
- 1 (8 ounce) package fresh mushrooms, sliced
- 2 tablespoons dried oregano
- 1 tablespoon Italian seasoning
- 2 teaspoons chili powder
- 1/4 cup brown sugar
- 1 (15 ounce) container ricotta cheese

Direction

- Bring a large pot of lightly salted water to a boil. Add tomatoes and cook for 10 minutes. Drain and rinse with cold water. Remove skins and return tomatoes to the pot and

- mash them. Stir in tomato paste and 2 cups water. Cover and simmer on low heat.
- Meanwhile, melt butter in a large skillet over medium heat. Sauté garlic and bay leaves for 1 minute, then stir in onions; sauté until onions are translucent. Stir in zucchini, green and red bell pepper and mushrooms. Slowly cook and stir for 5 to 7 minutes.
- Stir vegetables into tomato sauce and add oregano, Italian seasoning, chili powder and brown sugar. Simmer over low heat for 6 to 8 hours. Stir in the ricotta cheese 10 minutes before serving.

Nutrition Information

- Calories: 193 calories
- Total Fat: 11.2 g
- Cholesterol: 31 mg
- Sodium: 335 mg
- Total Carbohydrate: 19.1 g
- Protein: 7.4 g

Tomato Juice Spaghetti Sauce

"This is a sauce my cousin's mother-in-law made. I had it for the first time 5 1/2 years ago and haven't made anything else since."

SERVING: 12 | PREP: 30 M | COOK: 2 H | READY IN: 2 H 30 M

Ingredients

- 2 tablespoons olive oil
- 1 large onion, chopped
- 6 cloves garlic, chopped
- 1/2 teaspoon ground allspice
- 1 pinch ground cloves
- 1/4 teaspoon cayenne pepper, or to taste
- 1 1/2 fluid ounces white wine
- 2 (46 fluid ounce) cans tomato juice
- 3 (6 ounce) cans tomato paste
- 1 tablespoon white sugar
- 1 teaspoon dried oregano
- salt and pepper to taste

Direction

- Heat oil in a large pot over medium heat. Sauté onions and garlic until lightly browned. Season with allspice, cloves and cayenne. Stir in wine, and cook until liquid is reduced. Add tomato juice, tomato paste and sugar. Season with oregano, salt and pepper; bring to a boil. Reduce heat, and simmer 90 minutes, or until thickened.

Nutrition Information

- Calories: 107 calories
- Total Fat: 2.6 g
- Cholesterol: 0 mg
- Sodium: 914 mg
- Total Carbohydrate: 20.2 g
- Protein: 3.7 g

Tomato Sauce

"Simple spicy tomato sauce from scratch for multiple dinners."

SERVING: 12 | PREP: 15 M | COOK: 1 H | READY IN: 1 H 15 M

Ingredients

- 6 1/4 pounds tomatoes, crushed
- 1/2 cup extra virgin olive oil
- 1 1/2 tablespoons freshly ground black pepper
- 1 teaspoon chili seasoning mix
- 1 teaspoon salt
- 1 tablespoon minced onion
- 1 tablespoon dried oregano
- 1 tablespoon garlic powder
- 1 teaspoon finely minced fresh parsley
- 1 teaspoon white sugar

Direction

- In large saucepan over low heat, combine tomatoes, olive oil, pepper, chili seasoning, salt, onion, oregano, garlic powder, parsley and sugar. Simmer 1 hour. Serve.

Nutrition Information

- Calories: 134 calories
- Total Fat: 9.9 g
- Cholesterol: 0 mg
- Sodium: 229 mg
- Total Carbohydrate: 11.1 g

- Protein: 2.4 g

Vegan Lemon Arugula Pesto

"Made with arugula, olive oil, pine nuts, and nutritional yeast, this quick and easy vegan arugula pesto has a simple twist on the traditional pesto Genovese."

SERVING: 6 | PREP: 5 M | READY IN: 5 M

Ingredients

- 4 cups fresh arugula
- 2/3 cup olive oil
- 1/4 cup pine nuts
- 2 tablespoons nutritional yeast
- 2 cloves garlic
- 1 tablespoon lemon juice
- 1/2 teaspoon salt
- 1/4 teaspoon ground black pepper

Direction

- Combine arugula, olive oil, pine nuts, nutritional yeast, garlic, lemon juice, salt, and black pepper in the bowl of a food processor; pulse until smooth.

Nutrition Information

- Calories: 258 calories
- Total Fat: 27.1 g
- Cholesterol: 0 mg
- Sodium: 199 mg
- Total Carbohydrate: 2.7 g

- Protein: 3.1 g

Vegan Melanzane Eggplant Pasta Sauce

"A vegan version of a great Italian pasta sauce that showcases eggplant. Just stir in your favorite pasta once it's done!"

SERVING: 4 | PREP: 20 M | COOK: 20 M | READY IN: 40 M

Ingredients

- 1 tablespoon olive oil
- 1 onion, finely chopped
- 1 carrot, finely chopped
- 1 clove garlic, chopped
- 1 (14.5 ounce) can whole peeled tomatoes
- 1/2 teaspoon white sugar
- salt and ground black pepper to taste
- 1/2 cup vegetable oil for frying
- 1 eggplant, thinly sliced
- 2 tablespoons pitted Kalamata olives, sliced

Direction

- Heat olive oil in a saucepan over medium heat. Cook and stir onion, carrot, and garlic until onion is golden, about 5 minutes. Add tomatoes, sugar, salt, and pepper. Bring to a simmer; turn heat down to low. Continue simmering, stirring occasionally, for 10 minutes.
- Meanwhile, heat vegetable oil in a separate pan over high heat. Fry eggplant slices in the hot oil until lightly browned, about 2 minutes per side. Drain eggplant slices on paper towels.

- Mash the tomatoes in the saucepan using a fork for a less chunky texture. Remove from heat. Add eggplant and olives; stir gently to incorporate.

Nutrition Information

- Calories: 177 calories
- Total Fat: 10.4 g
- Cholesterol: 0 mg
- Sodium: 433 mg
- Total Carbohydrate: 21 g
- Protein: 3.2 g

Vegan Mushroom Bolognese

"Try this hearty and flavorful vegan alternative to the traditional Italian Bolognese sauce. It's perfect for serving over your favorite pasta, polenta, or even zucchini noodles."

SERVING: 4 | PREP: 20 M | COOK: 35 M | READY IN: 55 M

Ingredients

- 2 tablespoons olive oil
- 1 onion, chopped
- 1 medium carrot, diced
- 1 celery stalk, diced
- 2 cloves garlic, minced
- 2 cups button mushrooms, quartered
- 1 cup red wine
- 1 (14.5 ounce) can whole peeled tomatoes
- 1 tablespoon salt
- 1 teaspoon ground black pepper
- 1/2 teaspoon dried sage
- 3 bay leaves
- 1/2 teaspoon basil

Direction

- Heat olive oil in a skillet over medium heat; stir in onion. Cook and stir until the onion has softened and turned translucent, about 5 minutes. Add carrot, celery, and garlic; cook until soft, about 3 minutes. Add mushrooms; cook until tender, about 3 minutes. Pour in red wine; cook until wine has almost evaporated, about 3 minutes.

- Add tomatoes and season with salt, black pepper, sage, and bay leaves. Cook over medium-high heat and bring to a boil. Reduce heat to low and simmer, covered, about 20 minutes. Remove bay leaves and stir in basil.

Nutrition Information

- Calories: 162 calories
- Total Fat: 7.2 g
- Cholesterol: 0 mg
- Sodium: 1923 mg
- Total Carbohydrate: 12.8 g
- Protein: 3.1 g

Vegan Squash Pesto

"This is vegan pesto that is easy and delicious! Enjoy on bread or with any item!"

SERVING: 6 | PREP: 10 M | READY IN: 10 M

Ingredients

- 1 cup diced yellow squash
- 1 cup walnuts
- 1/2 cup fresh basil
- 1/2 cup fresh spinach
- 4 cloves peeled garlic
- 1/2 teaspoon pink salt
- 1/2 teaspoon cayenne pepper

Direction

- Blend yellow squash, walnuts, basil, spinach, garlic, salt, and cayenne pepper together in a blender until smooth.

Nutrition Information

- Calories: 118 calories
- Total Fat: 11 g
- Cholesterol: 0 mg
- Sodium: 197 mg
- Total Carbohydrate: 4.1 g
- Protein: 3.1 g

Vegan Sundried Tomato Pesto

"This pesto can be served over pasta (more than enough for 8 ounces). Mix with soy cream cheese, margarine, tofu for a spread."

SERVING: 3 | PREP: 30 M | READY IN: 30 M

Ingredients

- 2 cups fresh basil leaves
- 5 sun-dried tomatoes, softened
- 3 cloves garlic, crushed
- 1/4 teaspoon salt
- 3 tablespoons toasted pine nuts
- 1/4 cup olive oil

Direction

- Place basil, tomatoes, garlic, salt, and nuts in an electric food processor or blender. Puree. Add olive oil slowly, and blend slowly until the mixture is to your desired texture.

Nutrition Information

- Calories: 227 calories
- Total Fat: 22.7 g
- Cholesterol: 0 mg
- Sodium: 266 mg
- Total Carbohydrate: 4.8 g
- Protein: 3.6 g

White Wine And Garlic Dream Cream

"Don't even bother wasting your time making the usual boring alfredo!! Try this sauce and you'll never go back. The flavors are amazing and will impress any guest. One can never go wrong with white wine and garlic blended into a thick creamy peppery sauce."

SERVING: 3 | PREP: 15 M | COOK: 45 M | READY IN: 1 H

Ingredients

- 1 tablespoon butter
- 3 large shallots, sliced thinly
- 4 cloves garlic, chopped
- 1 1/2 cups white wine, divided
- ground white pepper to taste
- 3/4 cup heavy cream at room temperature
- 1 lemon, juiced
- salt to taste

Direction

- Melt butter in a medium saucepan over low heat. Cook and stir the shallots until they become translucent and tender; stir in garlic and cook until tender and aromatic.
- Stir in 1 cup white wine, increase heat to high and bring to a boil. Once it boils, add the remaining 1/2 cup wine. Boil for 10 minutes then reduce heat to medium-low. Season with white pepper to taste.
- When sauce is no longer boiling, slowly stir in cream, lemon juice and salt. Simmer for 3 to 5 minutes.

Nutrition Information

- Calories: 391 calories
- Total Fat: 26 g
- Cholesterol: 92 mg
- Sodium: 64 mg
- Total Carbohydrate: 18.5 g
- Protein: 3.3 g

Yummy Vegan Pesto Classico

"This is a classic recipe I use and love. Nutritional yeast is substituted for the traditionally used dairy. Tasty on pasta, bread, sandwiches, omelets, etc. Try adding sun-dried tomato slices post-completion for an added boost of rich flavor. P.S. - It also freezes beautifully."

SERVING: 16 | PREP: 15 M | READY IN: 15 M

Ingredients

- 1/3 cup pine nuts
- 2/3 cup olive oil
- 5 cloves garlic
- 1/3 cup nutritional yeast
- 1 bunch fresh basil leaves
- salt and pepper to taste

Direction

- Place the pine nuts in a skillet over medium heat, and cook, stirring constantly, until lightly toasted.
- Gradually mix the pine nuts, olive oil, garlic, nutritional yeast, and basil in a food processor, and process until smooth. Season with salt and pepper.

Nutrition Information

- Calories: 106 calories
- Total Fat: 10.6 g
- Cholesterol: 0 mg

- Sodium: 1 mg
- Total Carbohydrate: 1.7 g
- Protein: 2.2 g

Chapter 6: Amazing And Tasty Pasta Sauces

Amazing Sundried Tomato Cream Sauce

"This is a recipe I've created myself - and everyone that tries it loves it. It tastes just like at a restaurant and it can be made in the amount of time that it takes to cook pasta!"

SERVING: 4 | PREP: 5 M | COOK: 10 M | READY IN: 15 M

Ingredients

- 1 cup heavy cream
- 3 tablespoons butter
- 1/2 cup shredded mozzarella cheese
- 2 tablespoons grated Parmesan cheese
- 1/4 cup chopped sun-dried tomatoes
- salt and pepper to taste
- 1 tablespoon pine nuts

Direction

- Heat the cream and butter in a saucepan over medium heat until almost boiling, but do not boil. Add mozzarella and Parmesan cheeses, and stir until melted. Stir in the sun-dried tomatoes, and season with salt and pepper. Remove from heat and serve over pasta with a sprinkling of pine nuts.

Nutrition Information

- Calories: 349 calories
- Total Fat: 34.8 g
- Cholesterol: 116 mg
- Sodium: 280 mg
- Total Carbohydrate: 4.3 g
- Protein: 6.7 g

Artichoke Spinach Pasta Sauce

"A yummy dish I came up with over a batch of spinach artichoke dip. Serve over hot pasta immediately with French bread. If you prefer a pasta sauce that is not so chunky, process artichokes in food processor. Instead of a 1/2 cup of water use 1 cup water or add a second jar of Alfredo sauce."

SERVING: 8 | PREP: 20 M | COOK: 10 M | READY IN: 30 M

Ingredients

- 1/2 (13.5 ounce) can chopped spinach
- 1 (16 ounce) jar Alfredo sauce
- 1 (14 ounce) can artichoke hearts, drained and chopped
- 1/2 cup shredded mozzarella cheese
- 1/3 cup shredded Parmesan cheese
- 1/4 (8 ounce) package cream cheese, softened
- 2 cloves garlic, chopped
- 1 Roma tomato, diced (optional)
- 1/2 cup water

Direction

- Puree spinach in food processor until smooth.
- Whisk spinach, Alfredo sauce, artichoke hearts, mozzarella cheese, Parmesan cheese, cream cheese, garlic, and tomato together in a pot.
- Pour water into Alfredo sauce jar and top with lid. Shake water in jar to release last remnants of Alfredo sauce, and stir into pot with Alfredo sauce mixture.

- Cook Alfredo sauce mixture over medium heat, stirring occasionally, until cheeses have melted and sauce is bubbling, 10 to 15 minutes.

Nutrition Information

- Calories: 247 calories
- Total Fat: 21.2 g
- Cholesterol: 38 mg
- Sodium: 855 mg
- Total Carbohydrate: 8.1 g
- Protein: 8.2 g

Beef And Eggplant Sauce For Pasta

"This eggplant sauce is my family's favorite. I had a bumper crop of eggplant so have made up my own recipes using eggplant. Serve over your favorite pasta."

SERVING: 16 | PREP: 15 M | COOK: 29 M | READY IN: 44 M

Ingredients

- olive oil, divided
- 2 small eggplants, diced with skin
- 1 large red onion, chopped
- 1 (5 ounce) can sliced mushrooms, drained, or to taste
- 4 cloves garlic, minced, or more to taste
- 6 Roma tomatoes, sliced
- 2 pounds ground beef
- 2 cups pasta sauce (such as Hunt's® Traditional)
- 1 (15 ounce) can tomato sauce
- 1 (14 ounce) can pizza sauce
- 1/4 cup white sugar, or more to taste
- 1 (1.5 ounce) envelope dry spaghetti sauce mix
- salt and ground black pepper to taste

Direction

- Heat 1 tablespoon olive oil in a large pot over medium-high heat. Sauté eggplants, red onion, mushrooms, and garlic until softened, 8 to 10 minutes.
- Heat remaining 1 tablespoon olive oil in a skillet over medium-high heat. Sauté tomatoes until juicy and tender, about 6 minutes. Transfer tomatoes to the pot.

- Cook and stir ground beef in the same skillet until browned and crumbly, 5 to 7 minutes. Transfer to the pot; add pasta sauce, tomato sauce, pizza sauce, sugar, spaghetti sauce mix, salt, and pepper. Stir and simmer until flavors are well blended, about 10 minutes.

Nutrition Information

- Calories: 221 calories
- Total Fat: 11.6 g
- Cholesterol: 35 mg
- Sodium: 706 mg
- Total Carbohydrate: 17.8 g
- Protein: 11.8 g

www.ingramcontent.com/pod-product-compliance
Lightning Source LLC
Chambersburg PA
CBHW071443070526
44578CB00001B/204